THE AMBASSADOR

STARLEE KINE

The greatest gift I have ever given was to my friend Heather's seven-year-old daughter. We went to the amusement park for the day, just her and I, and she asked if she could go bounce around on the giant trampoline. I told her, yes, and just as she was about to go in, she turned to me and asked if when she was done, she could go in again. I nodded, yes, again, and she jumped for joy. Being as it was on a trampoline, her jump for joy was rather impressive. She was like a fly let out of a jar after years of captivity, basking in the freedom that came with knowing the fun wouldn't end quite yet.

Jaimie Warren's photographs inspire a similar feeling. She takes anywhere from ten to a hundred pictures a day. The other morning, she took thirty pictures alone of "gross-looking food, like fucked-up looking omelettes before they are fully cooked." In her book *Slouching Towards Bethlehem*, part of what's so interesting about Joan Didion feeling sick of all the hippies is that she was feeling this in 1968. It's a rare person who can be so of her own time, and Jaimie Warren belongs firmly in this camp. It is also possible that she has actually come from the future, in order to show us all how to live in the present. The way she dresses in some of her shots is a lot like the way people in the seventies might have imagined we would all dress by now. Jaimie says that "dressing up funny" is a big part of her daily routine. She is the antithesis of the girl who shows up at the Halloween party in a sexy cat costume, or the girl who posts on Facebook the hottest picture of herself that has ever been taken, a photo that is in fact so hot that it looks nothing at all like her. There is a fine line between ironic detachment and utter sincerity, and as a viewer, sometimes the only way to tell the difference is by going with a feeling in the gut. Jaimie Warren's photographs make you feel included, not alienated. They are about finding the most unflattering angle of your face, pinpointing the light in which your chin looks the weakest, then embracing this knowledge with all your heart.

Jaimie lives in Kansas City, Missouri, and says she is often asked when she is going to leave. But Jaimie isn't going anywhere. She likes it there. I lived in Chicago for five years, before moving to New York. I knew a guy there who made homemade robot costumes out of detergent bottles. He wore them everywhere. Whenever I try and imagine what Jaimie Warren's inner voice sounds like, I think of this guy. I think of her walking through the streets of Kansas City, thinking her thoughts in my friend's voice. I imagine that she doesn't go looking for the fun at all; instead, it comes to her. She is waiting for her plane to take off and suddenly she understands that of course it's time to scream. She is in a store when she realizes that ketchup dispensers are the most fun to be had on earth. She's like Dorothy in the *Wizard of Oz*, when one by one all the Munchkins come out from their hiding places to greet her. Kansas City has been waiting for an ambassador like Jaimie Warren for as long as she's been waiting for a home like Kansas City.

Another question Jaimie is often asked is if her pictures can be classified as party photos. I personally think she should wear the label proudly. She is both observer and participant, which I didn't think was even possible. I thought it was like rival bank robbers–the town isn't big enough for the two of them. Jaimie, though, has brought the two sides together and her pictures reflect this. In order to be the person who can capture the party, you have to be the person who can enjoy it first.

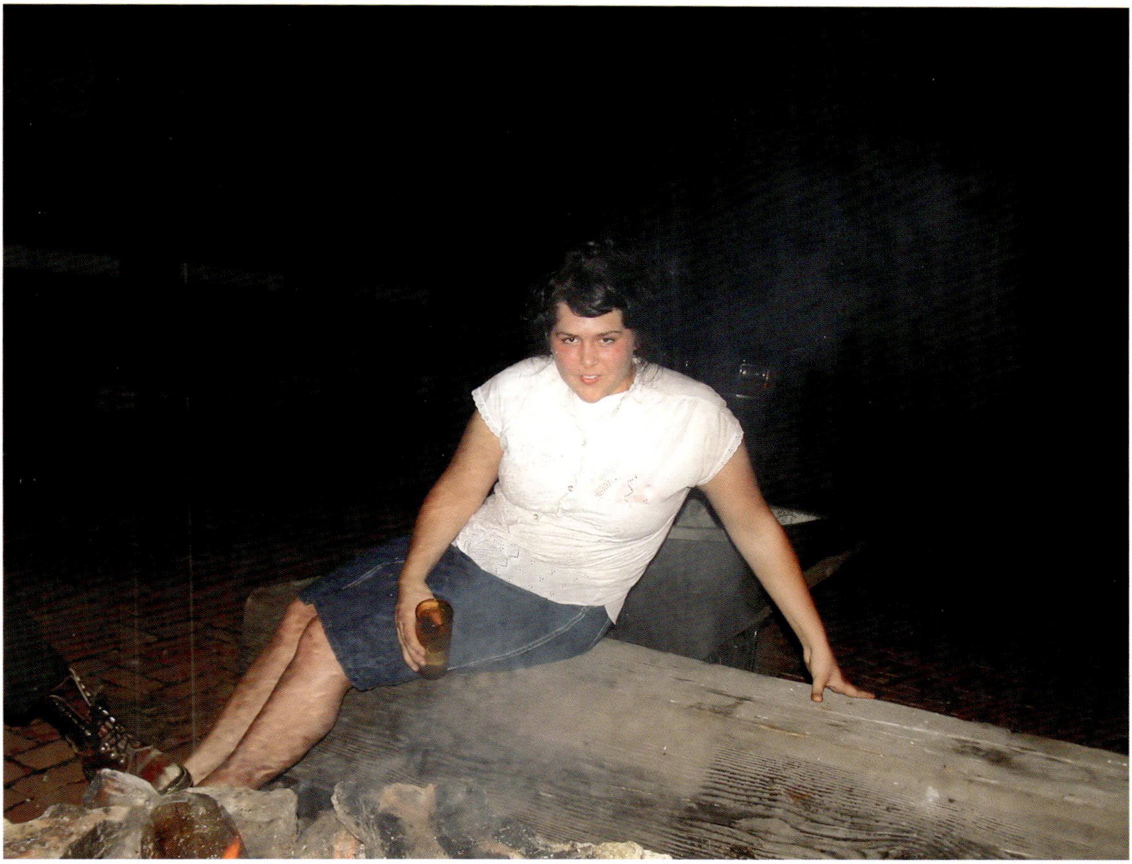

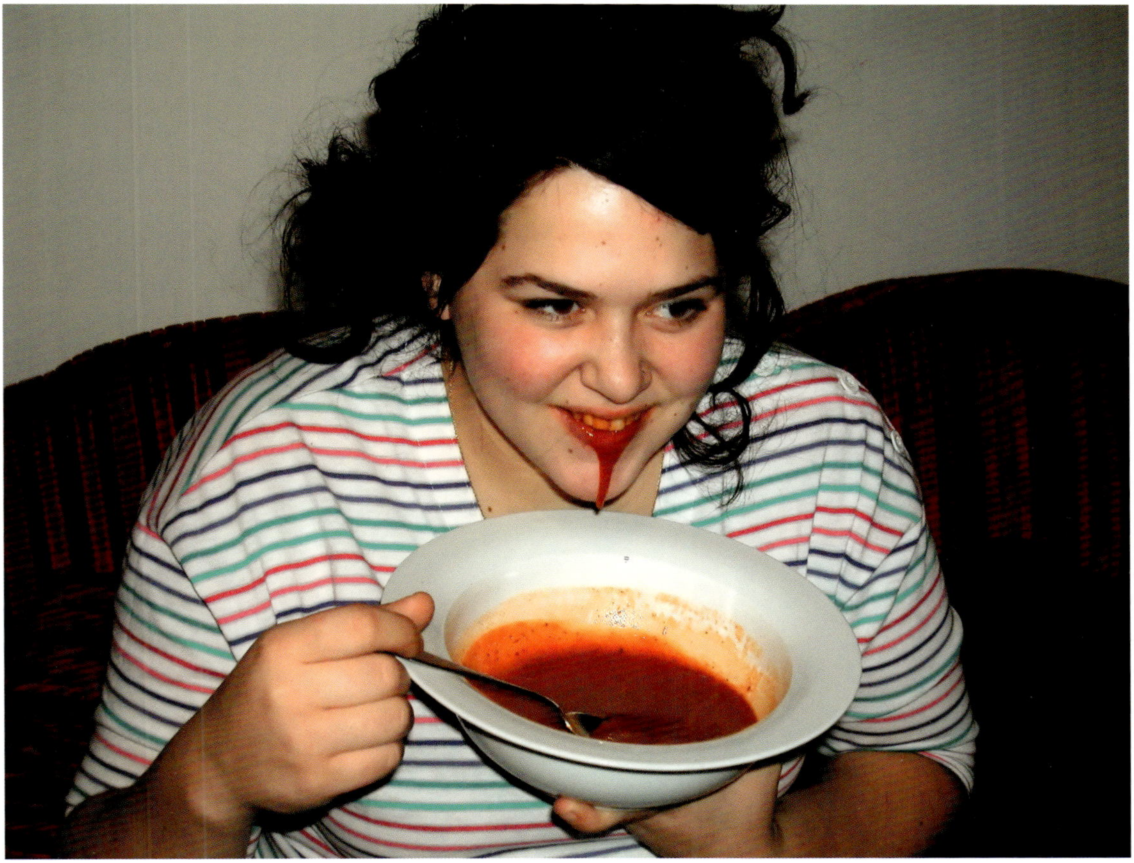

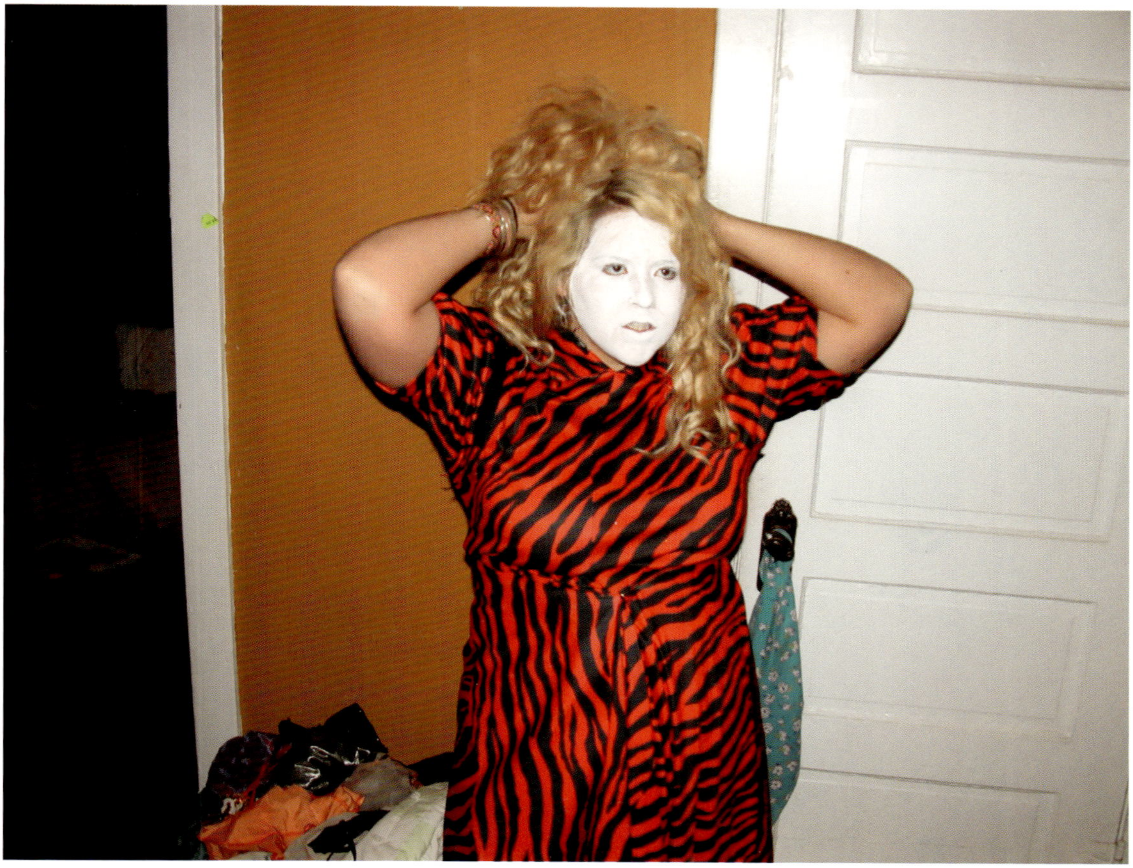

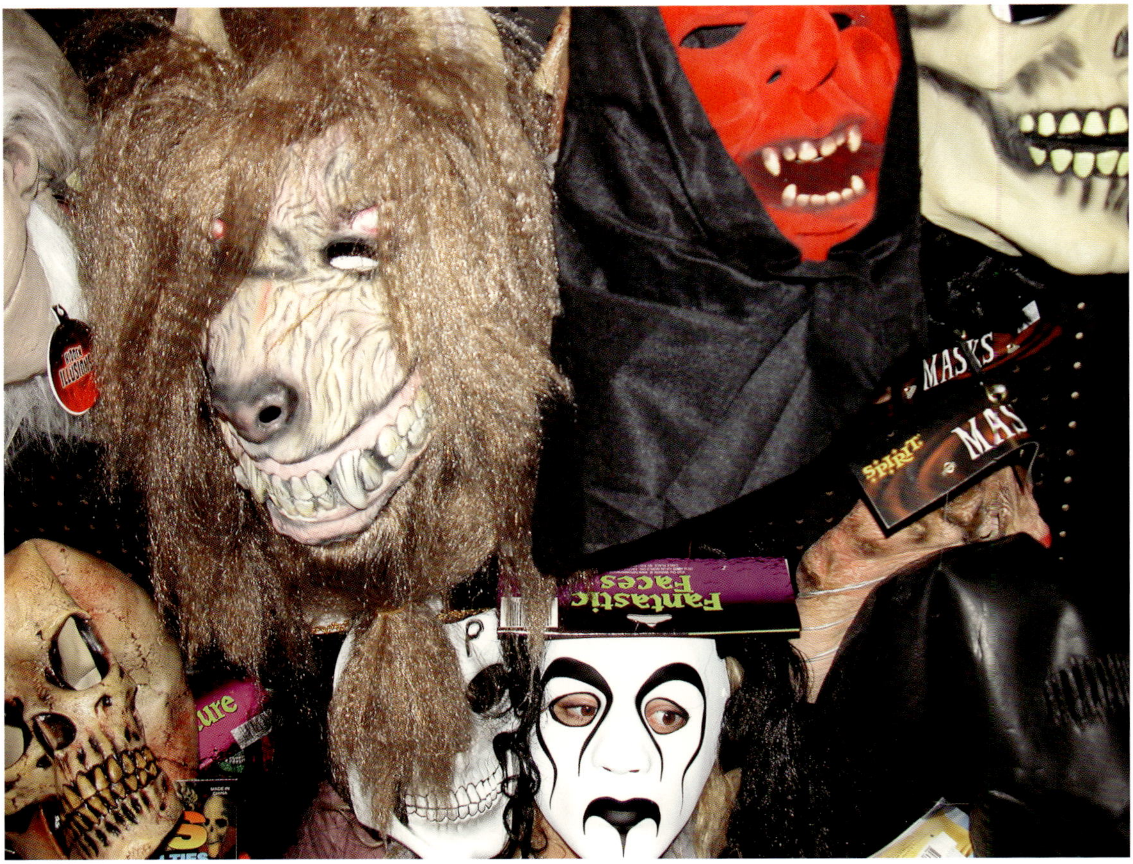
MASKS
SPIRIT
MASKS
Fantastic Faces

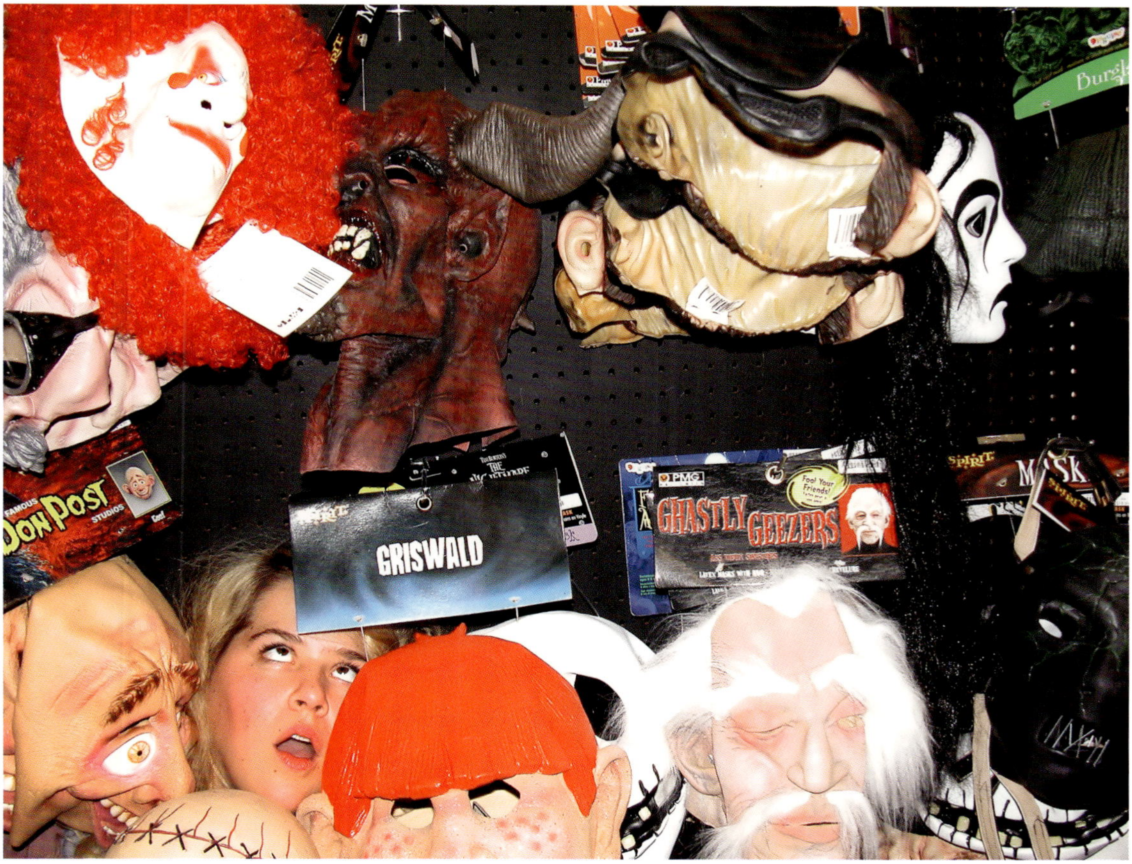
FAMOUS
DON POST
STUDIOS
GRISWALD
GHASTLY GEEZERS
PMG
Fool Your Friends!
SPIRIT
MASK

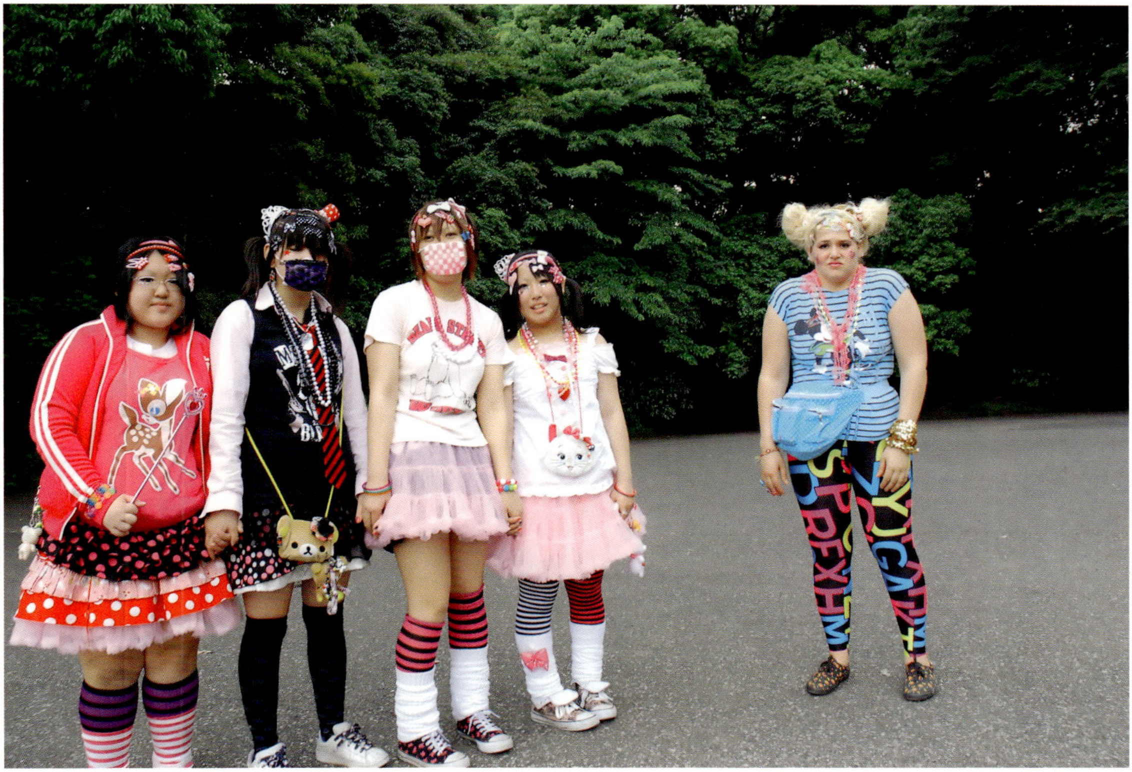

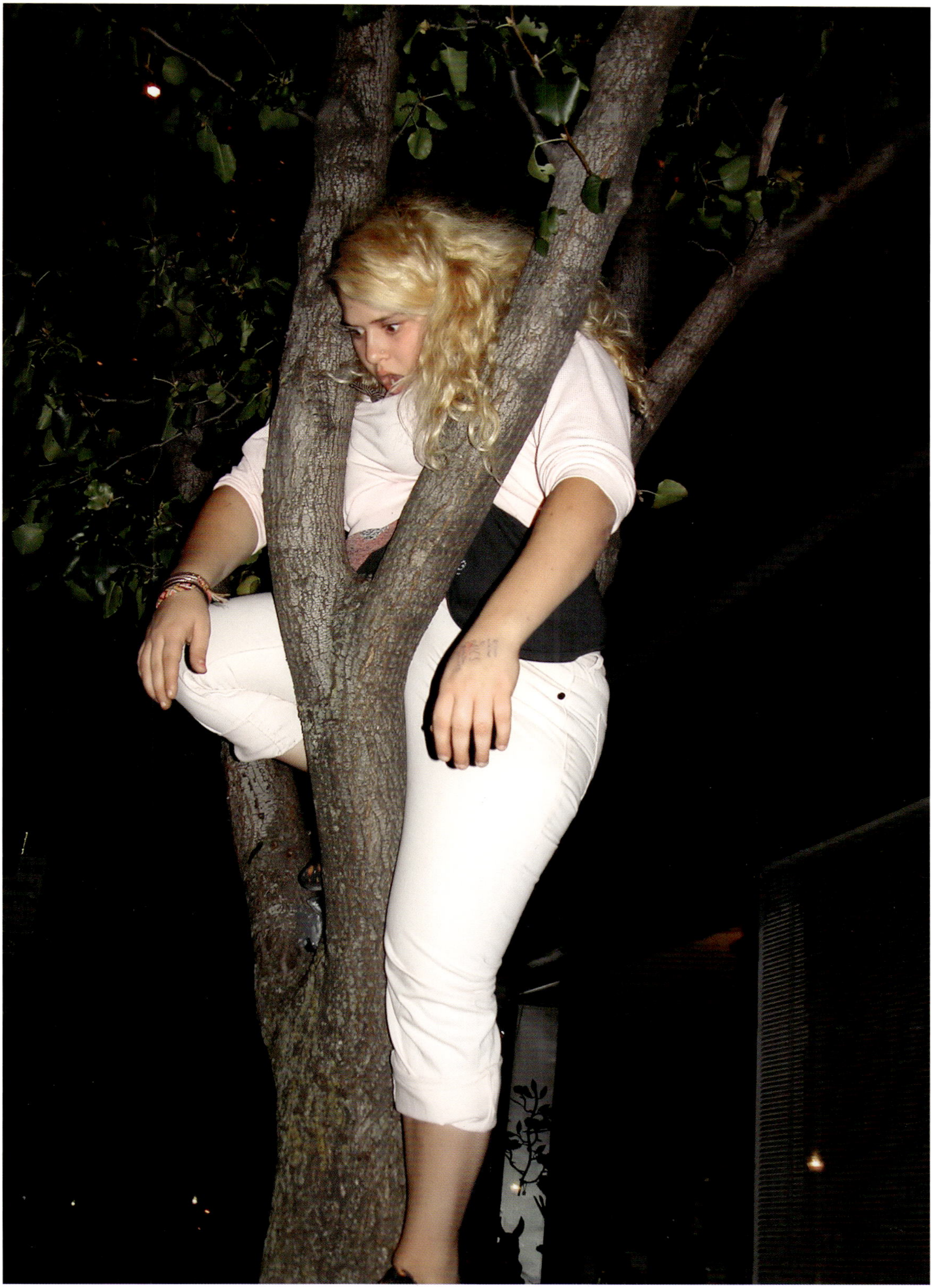

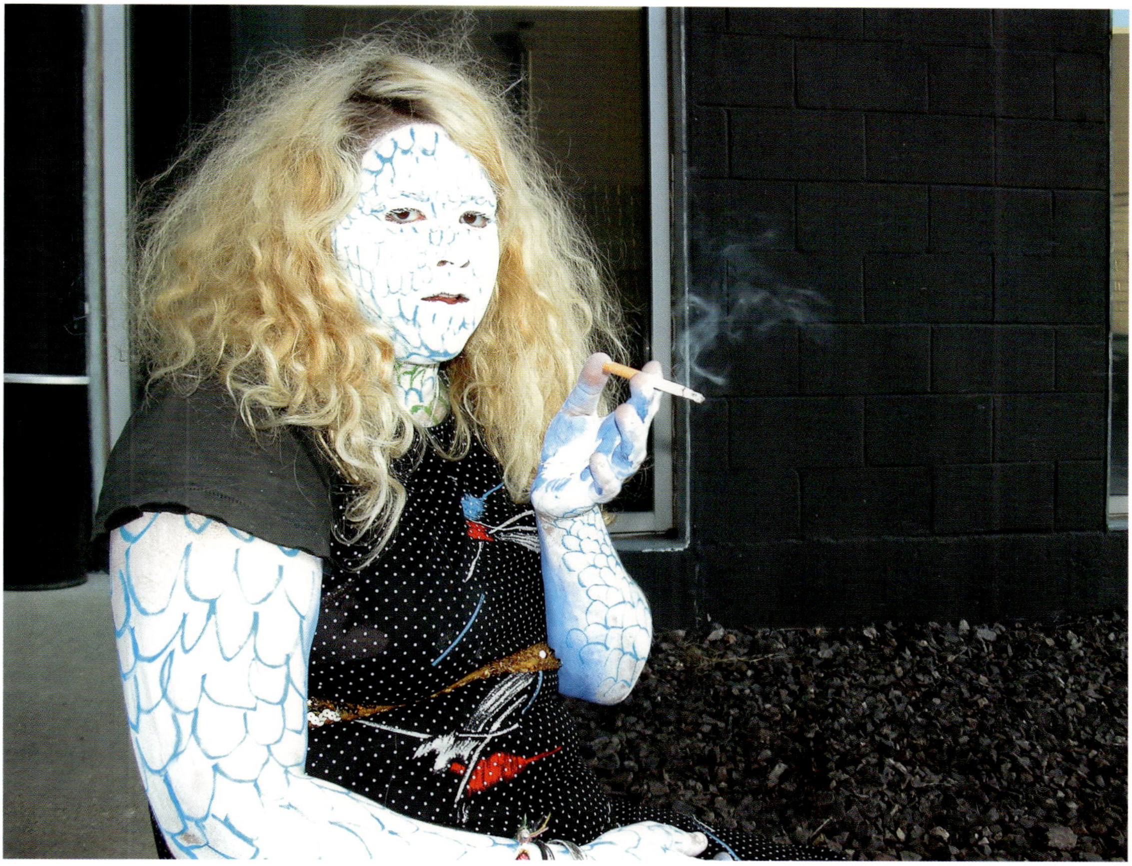

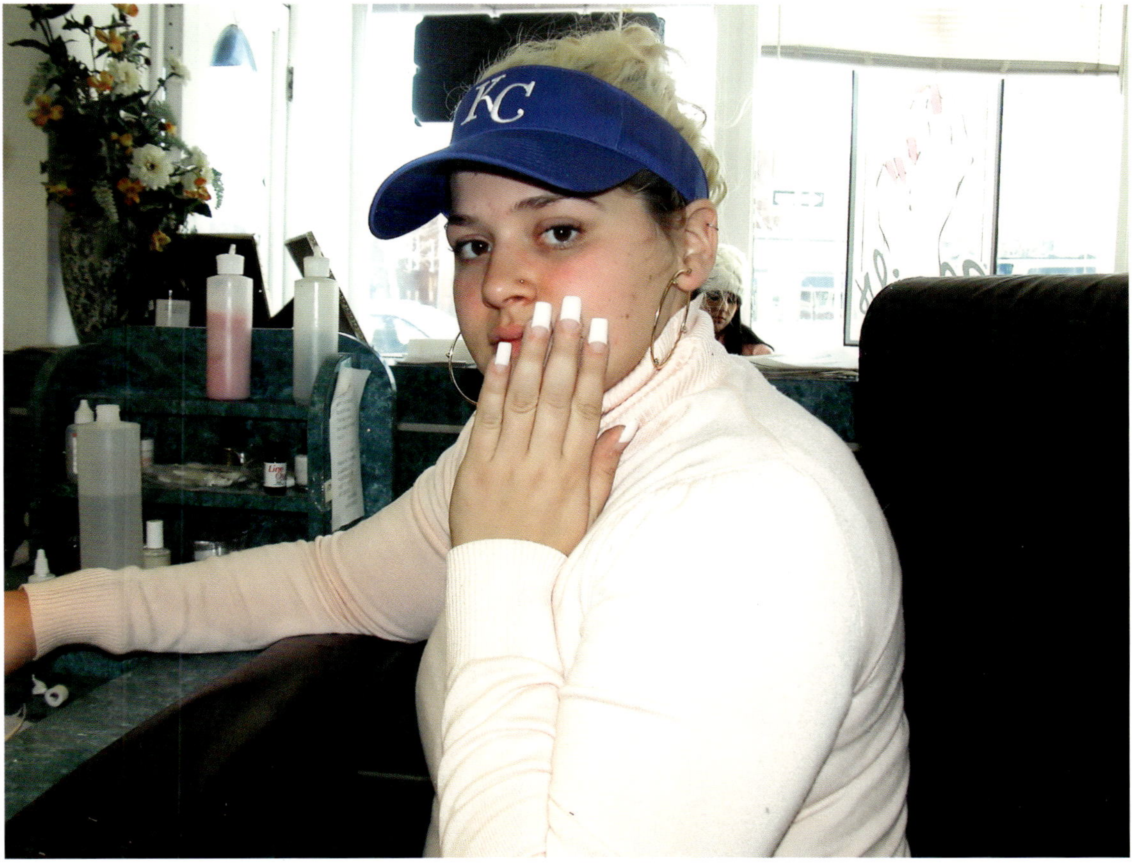
KC

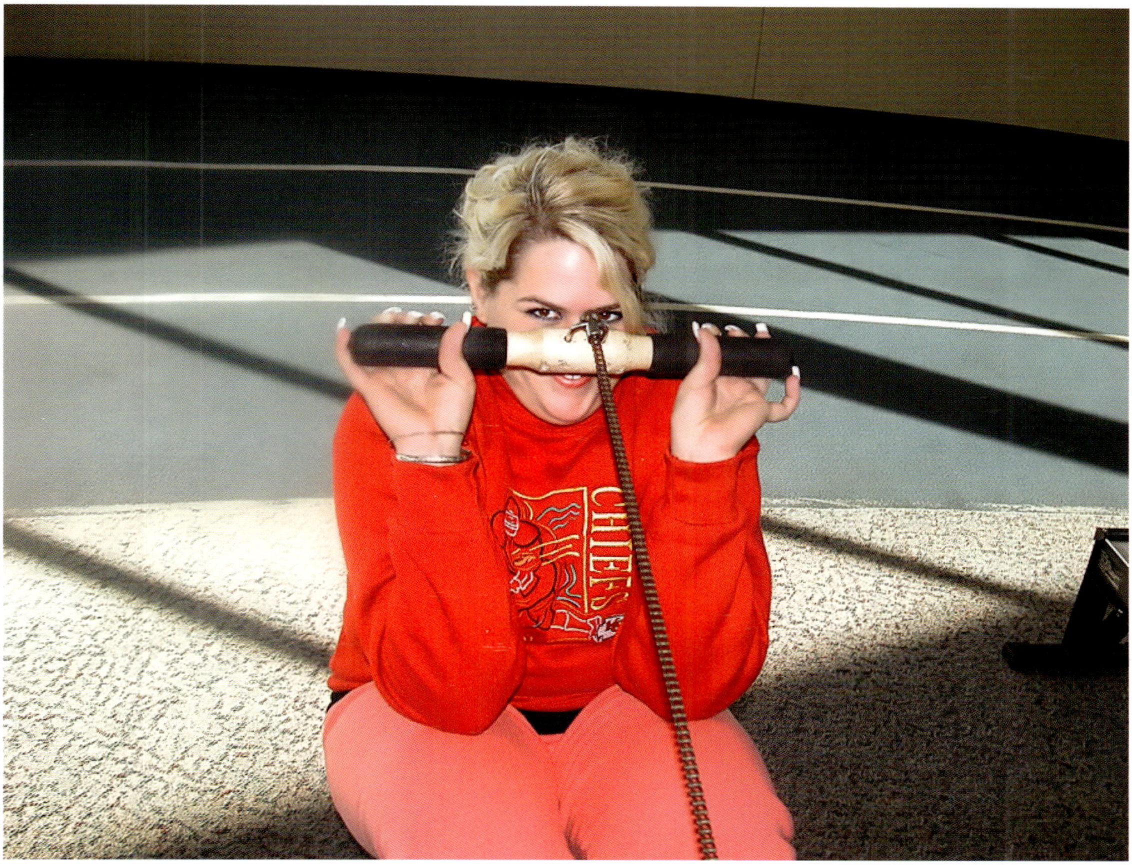
CHIEFS
CHIEFS

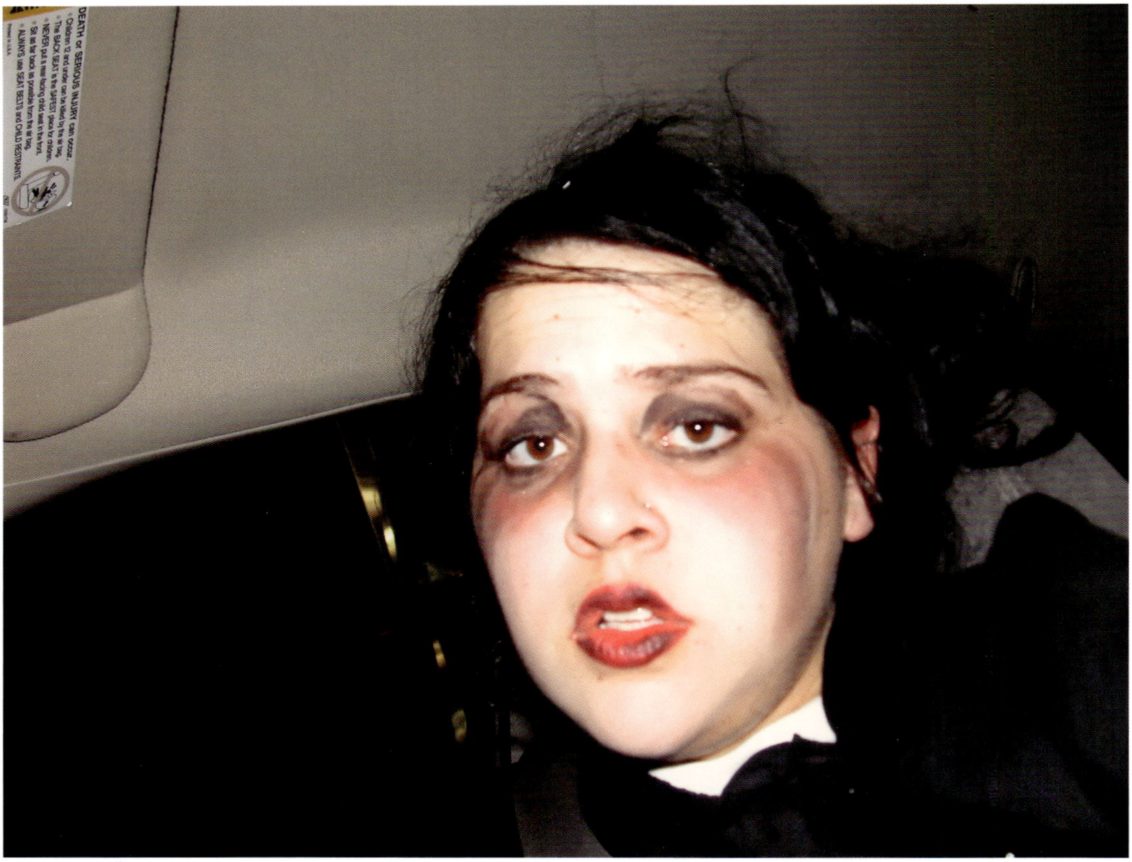
DEATH or SERIOUS INJURY can occur.
Children 12 and under can be killed by the air bag.
The BACK SEAT is the SAFEST place for children.
NEVER put a rear-facing child seat in the front.
Sit as far back as possible from the air bag.
ALWAYS use SEAT BELTS and CHILD RESTRAINTS.

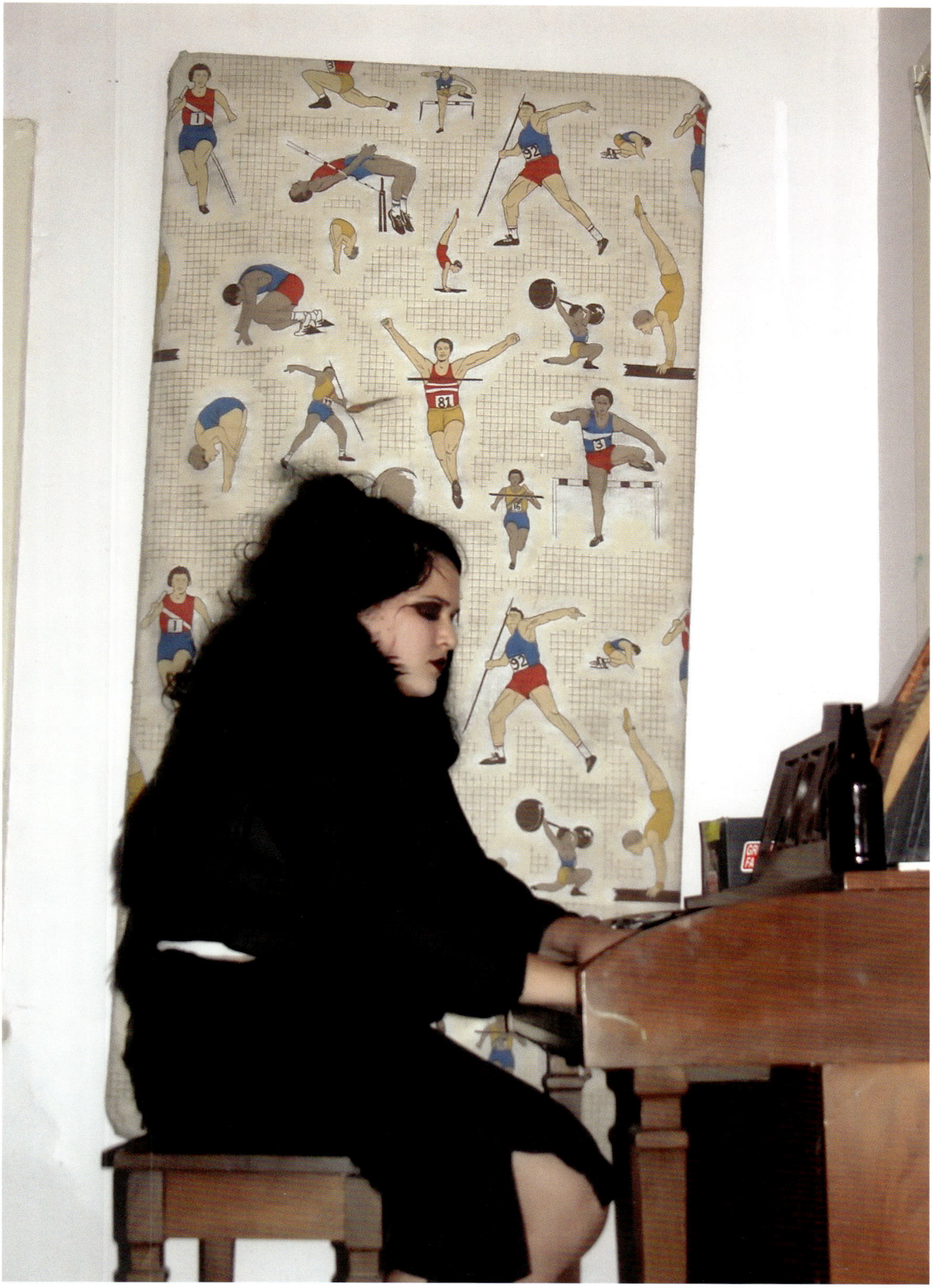

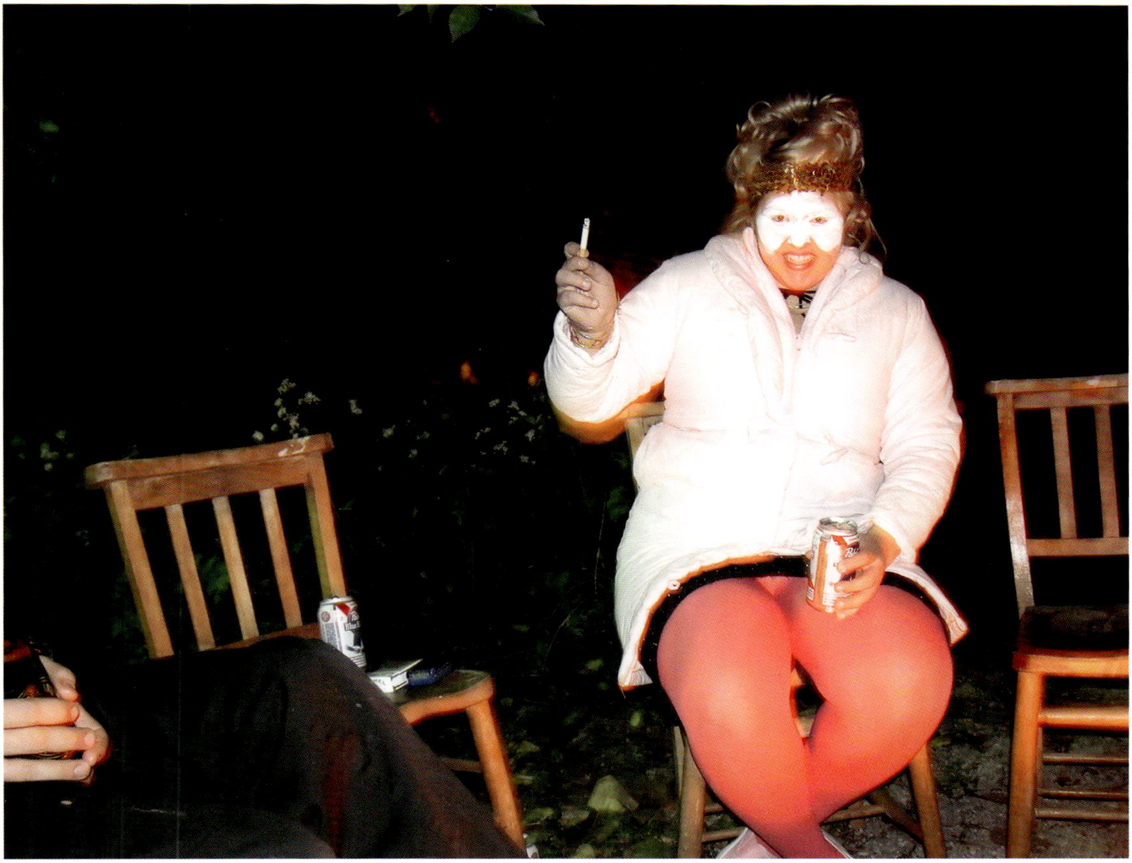

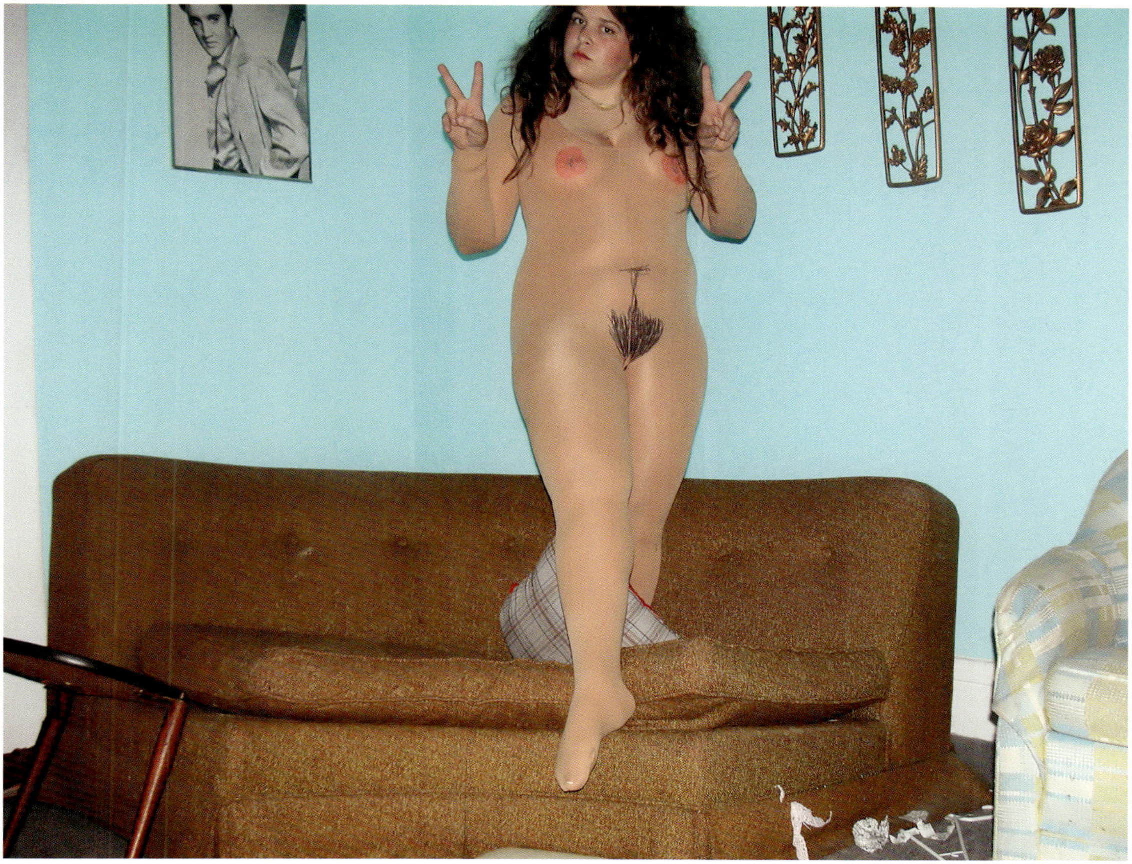

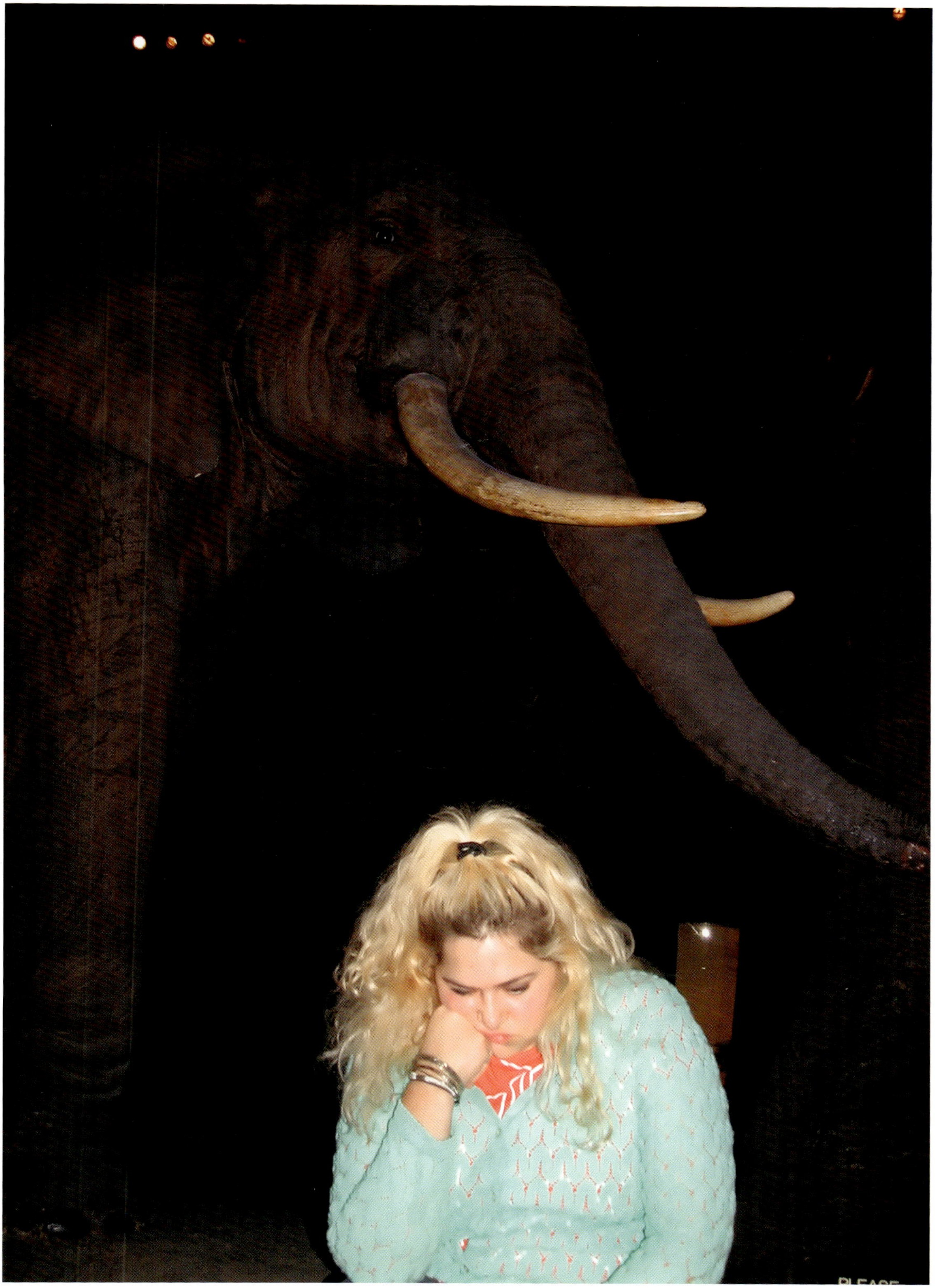

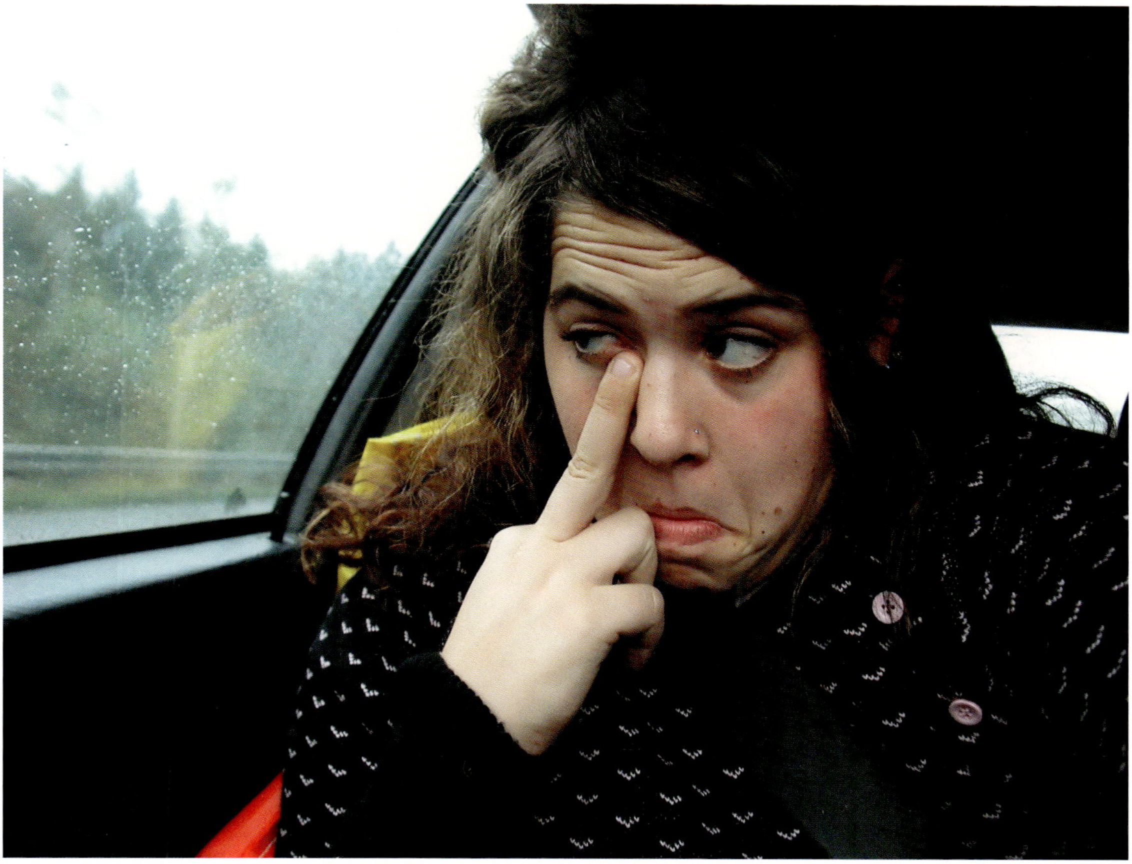

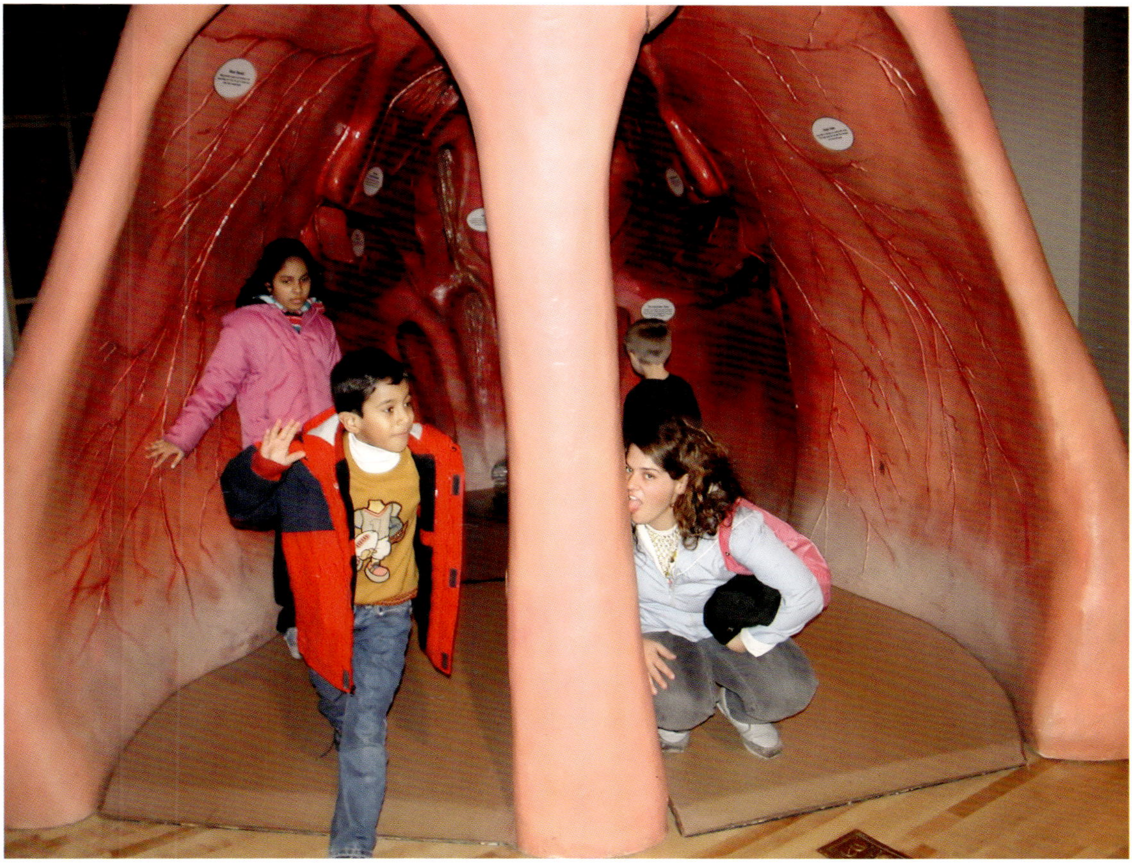

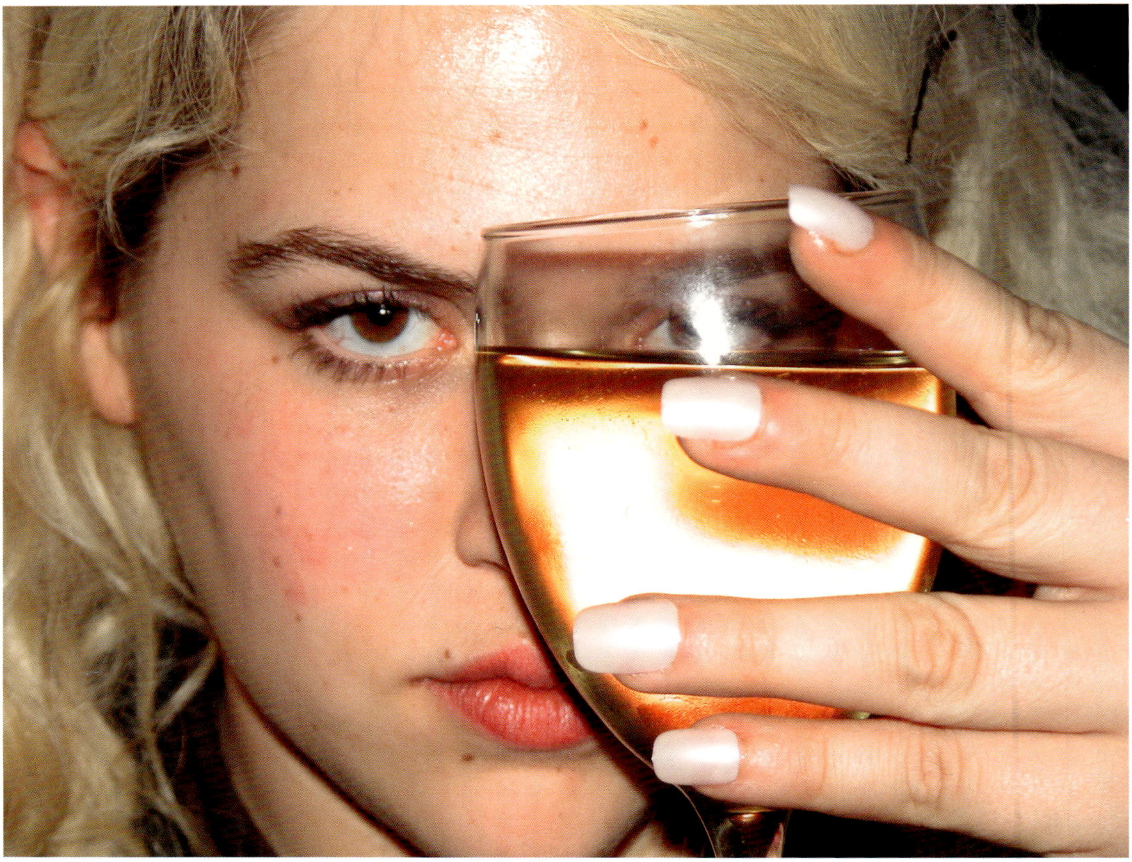

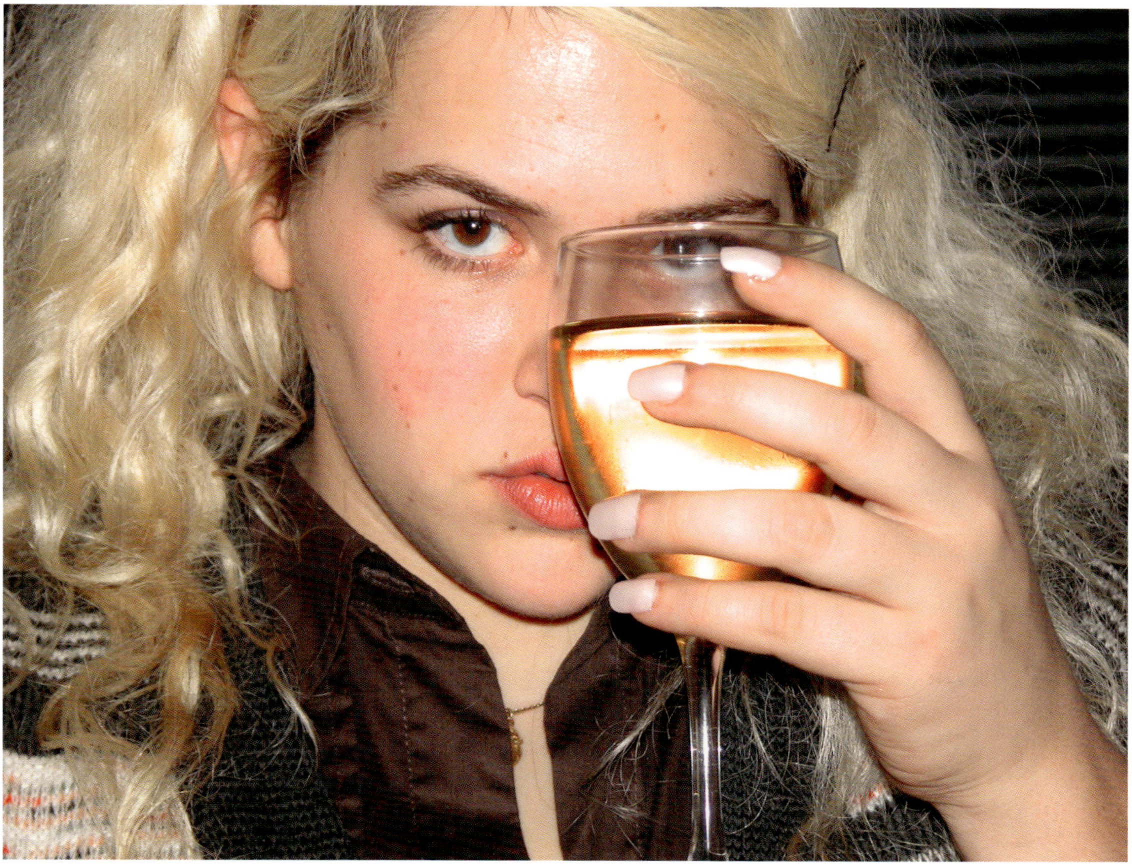

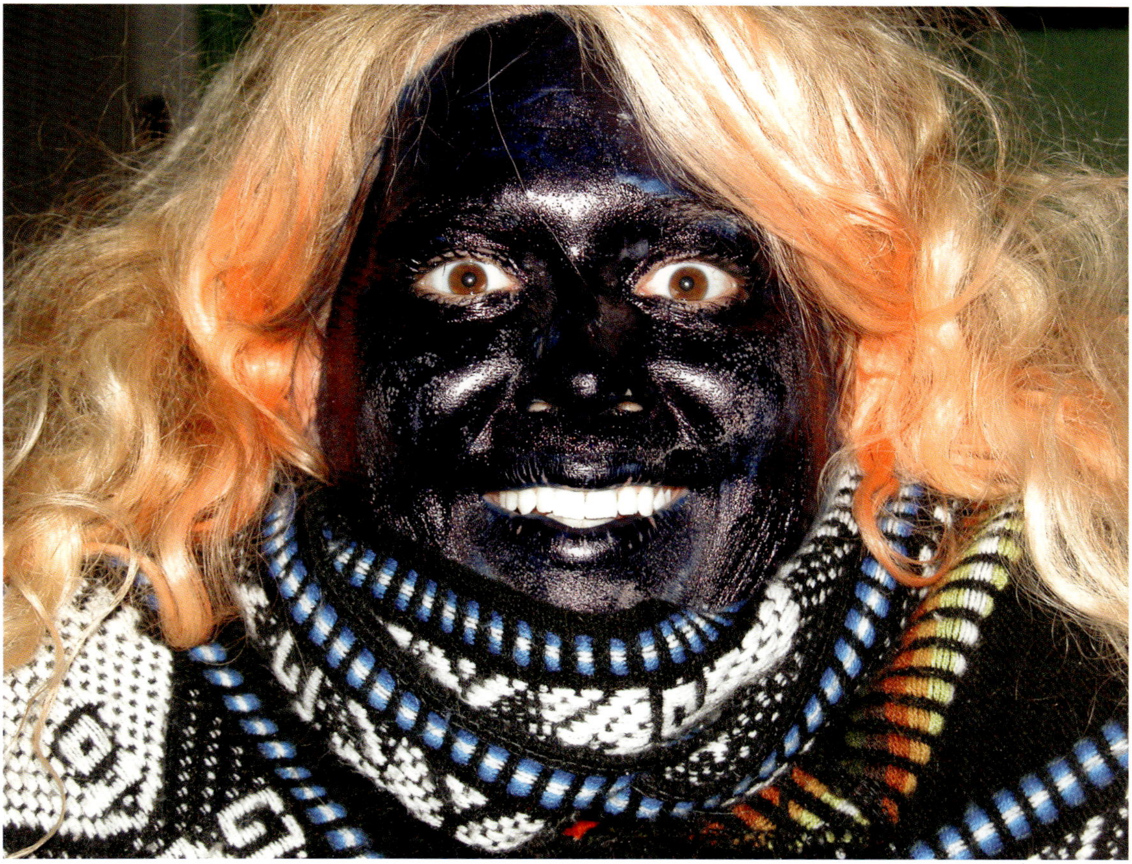

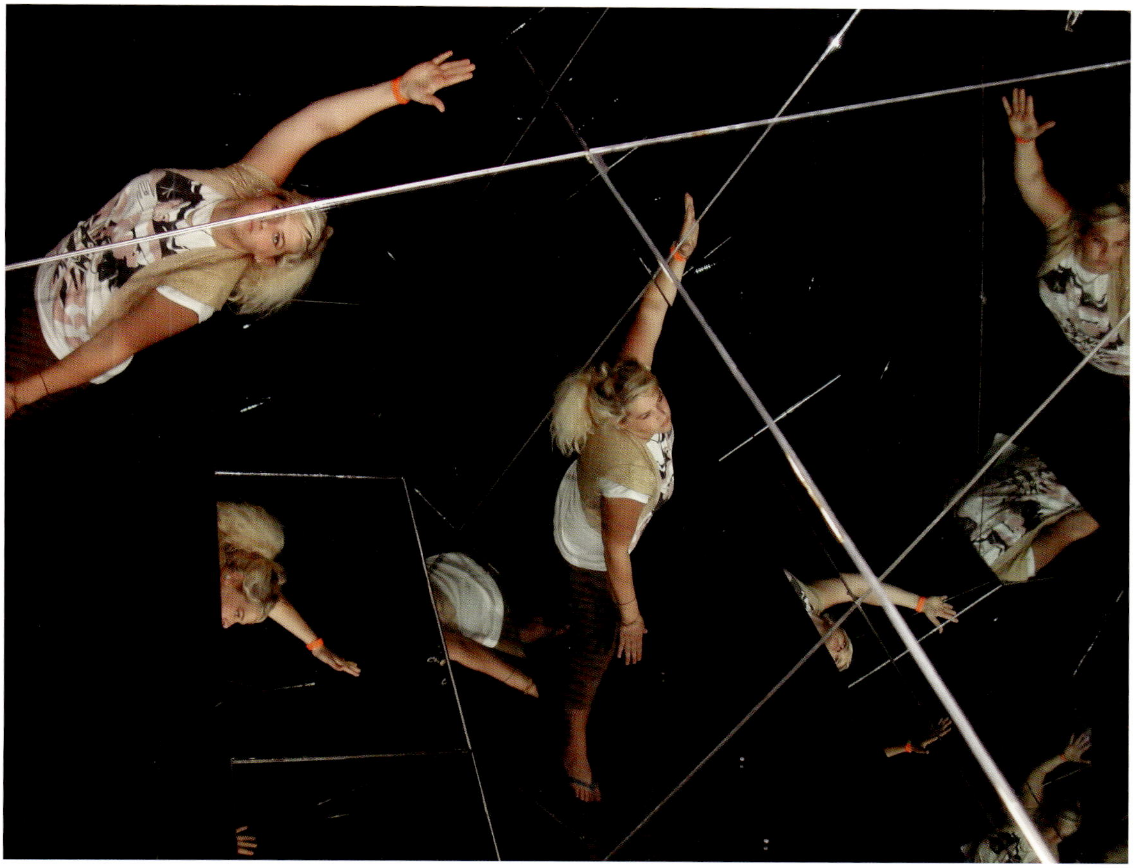

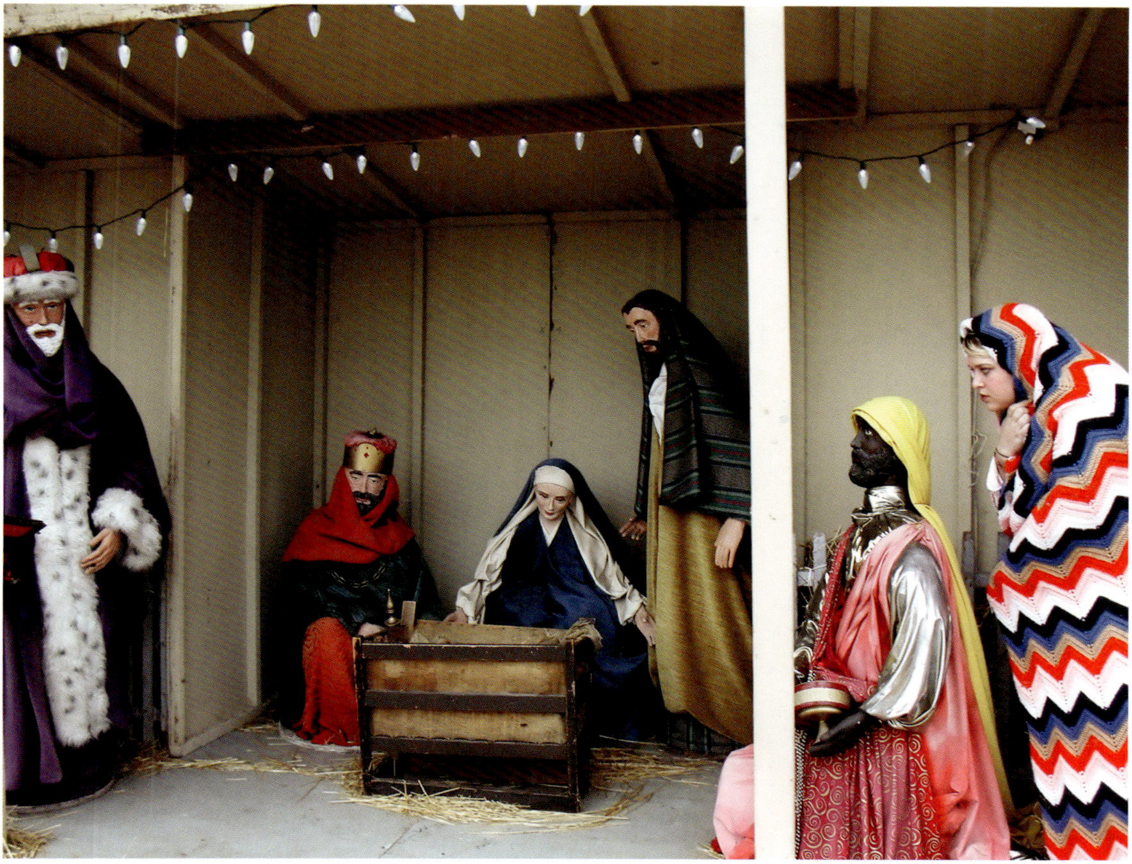

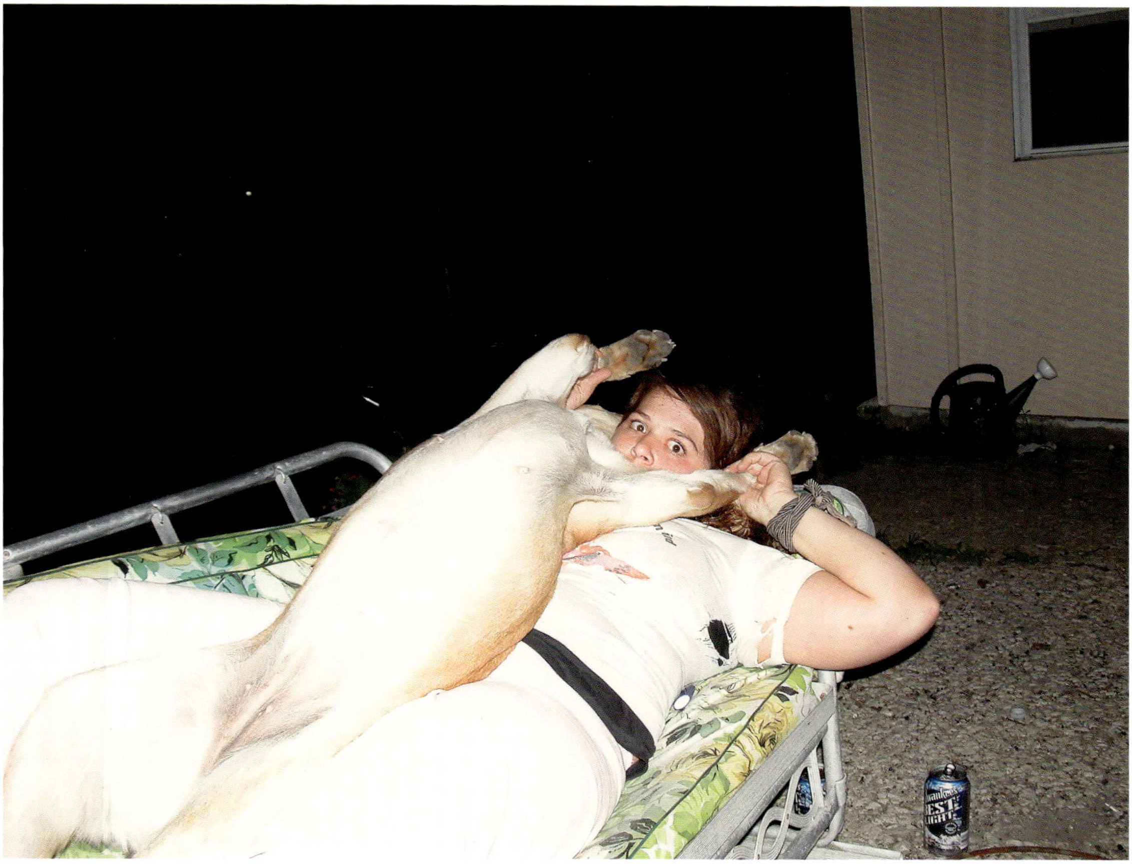

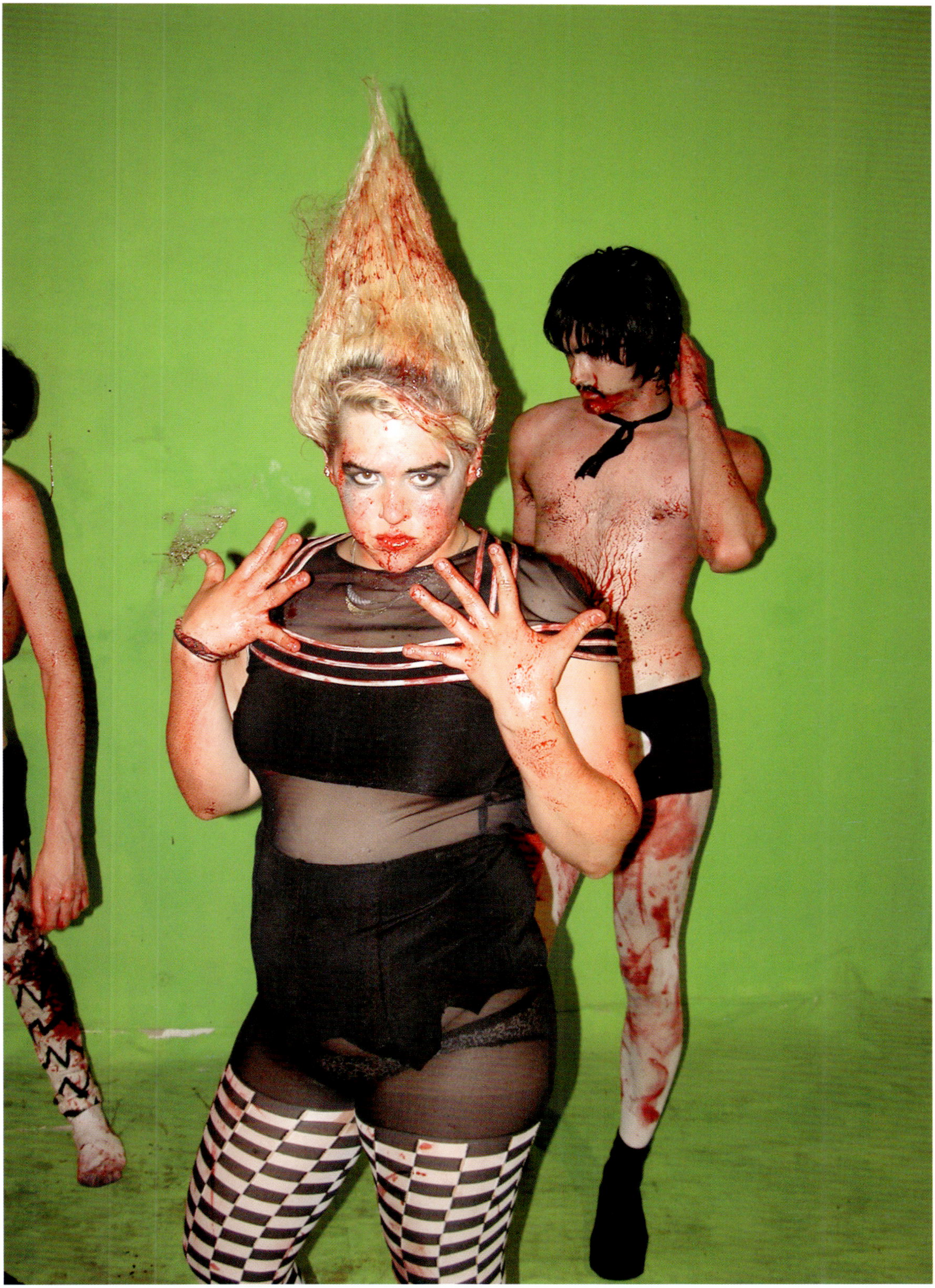

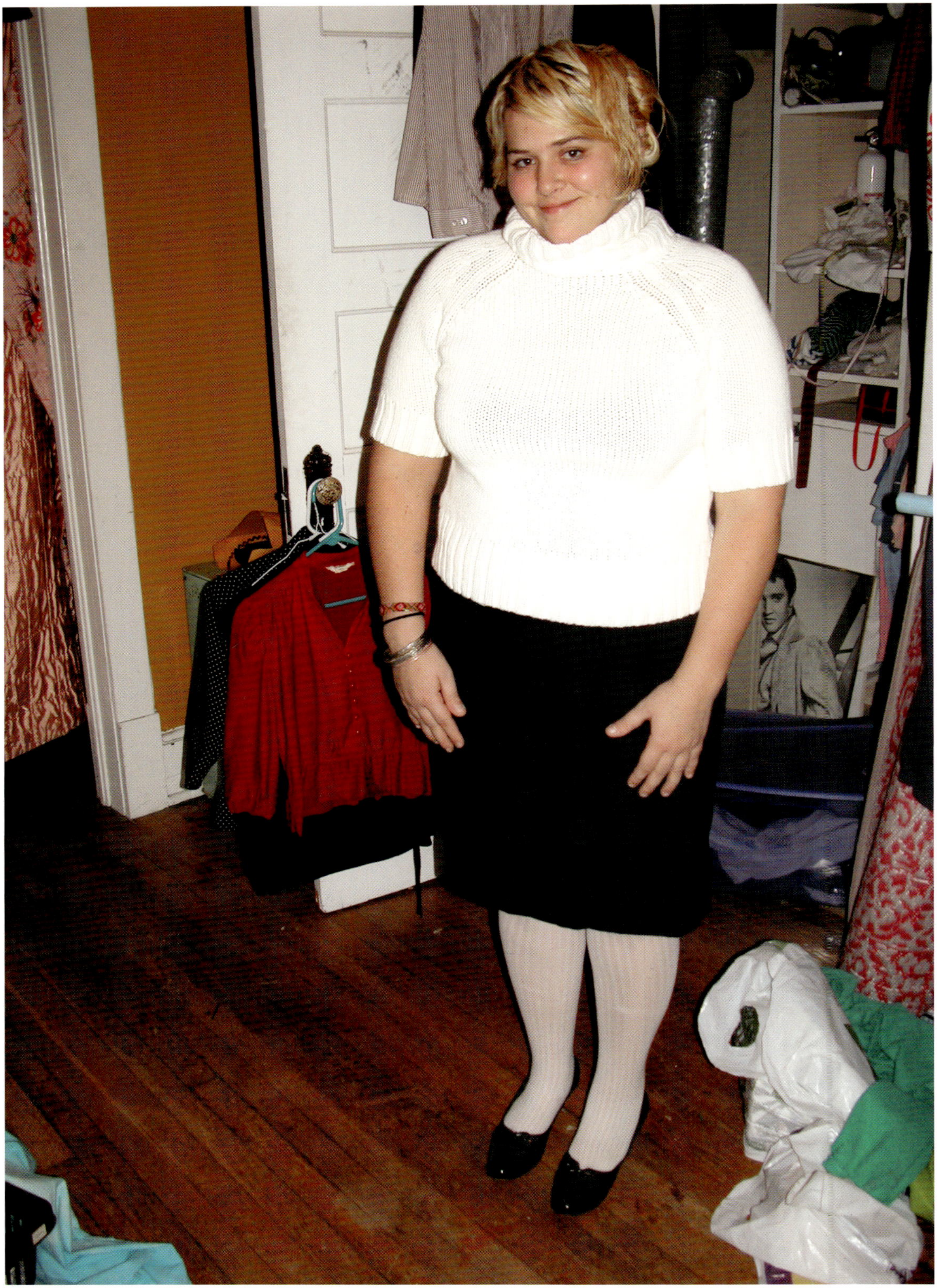

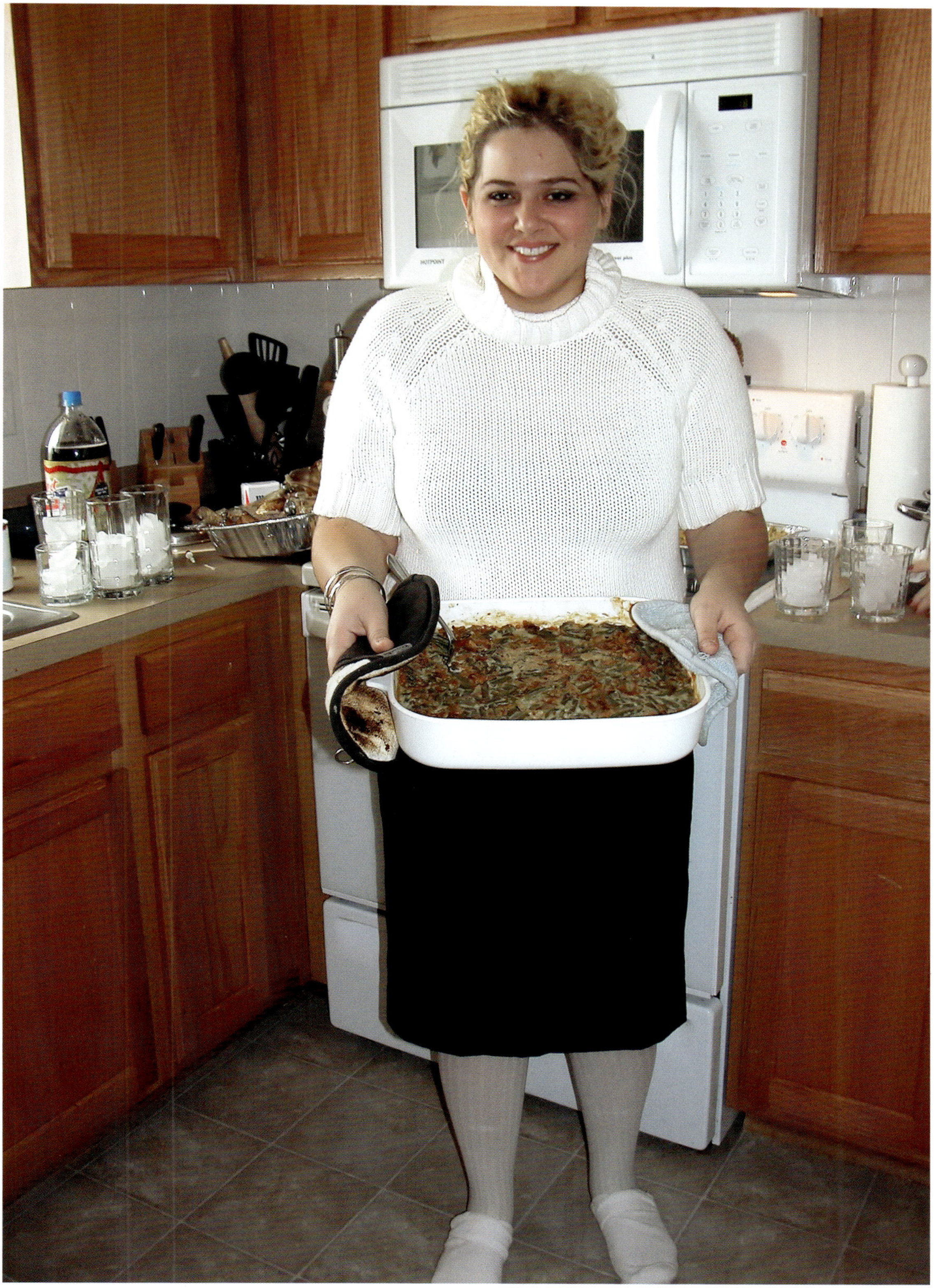
HOTPOINT

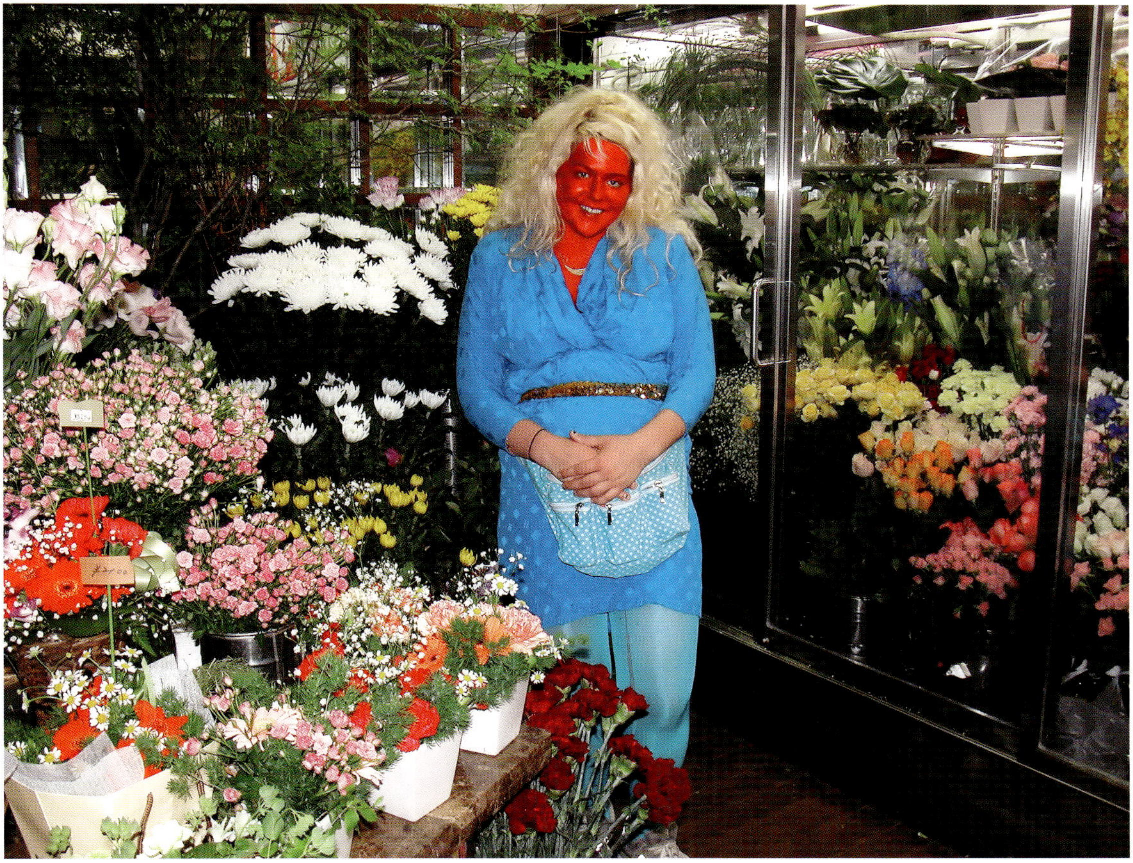

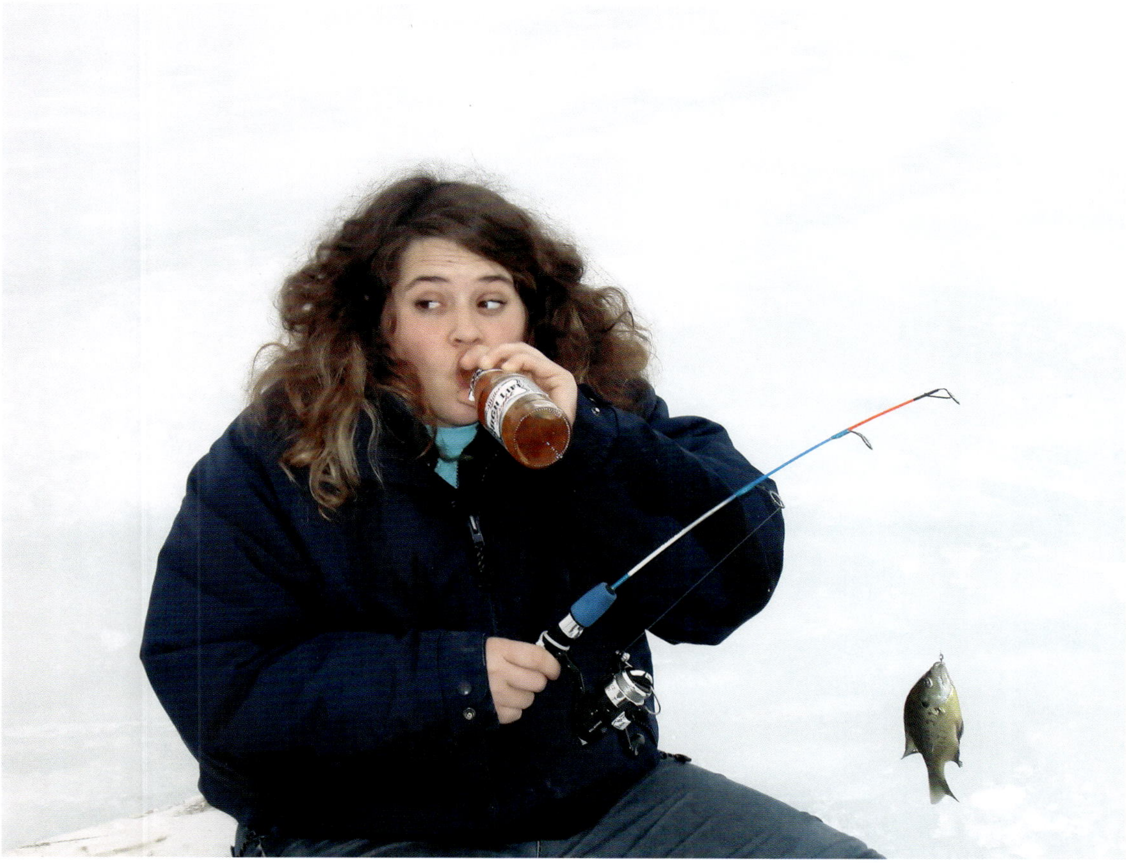

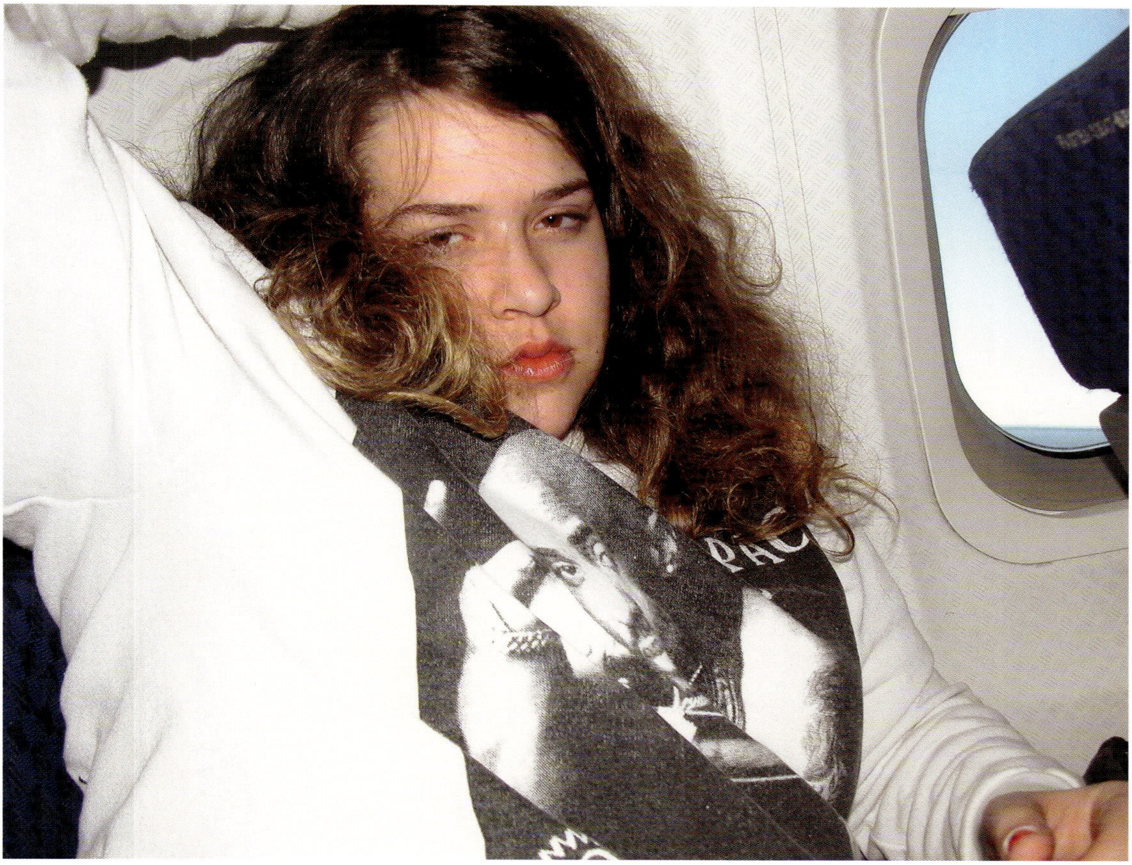

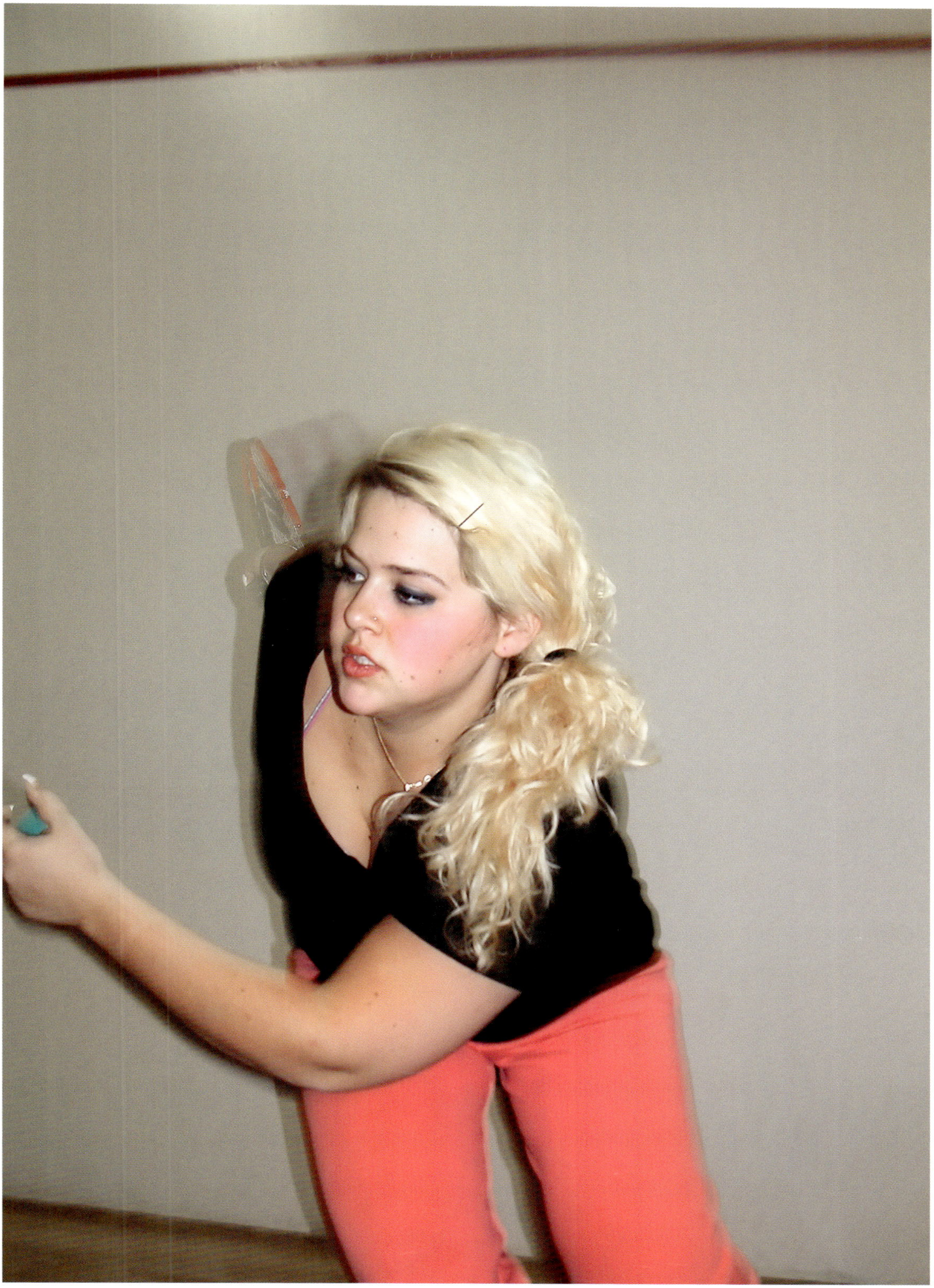

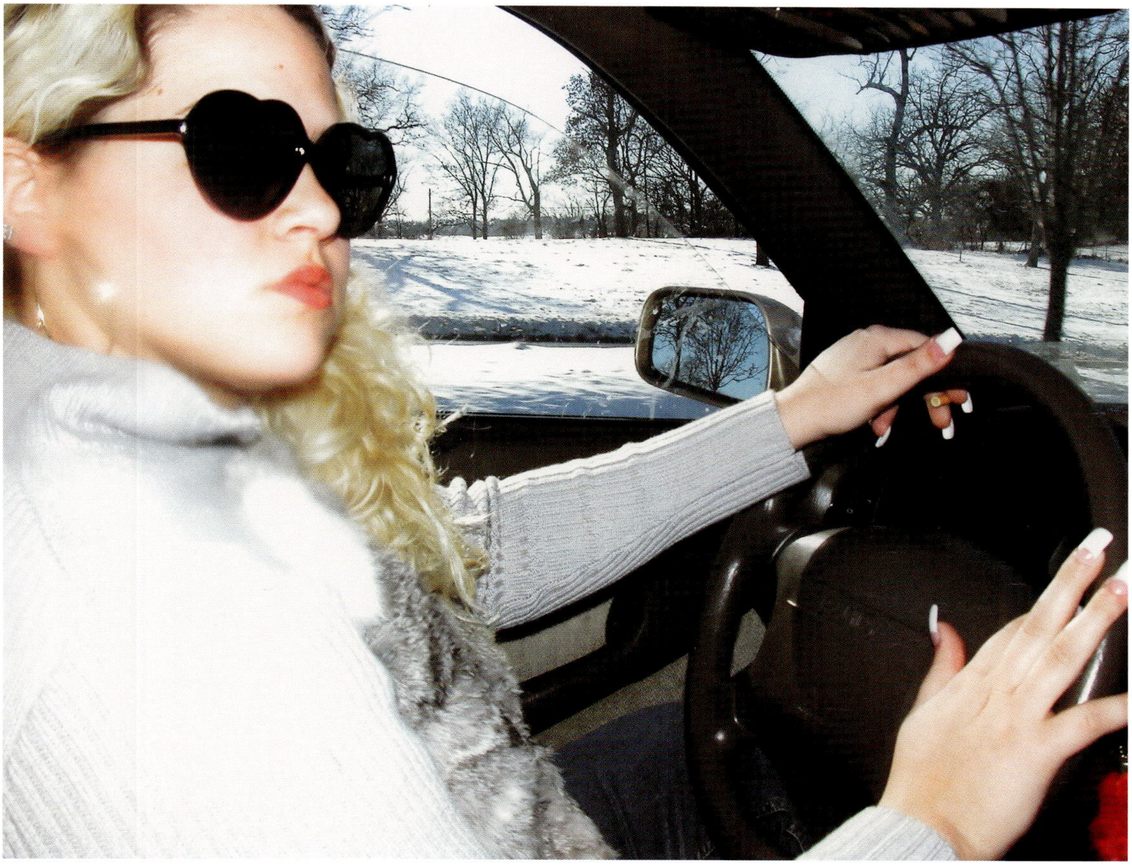

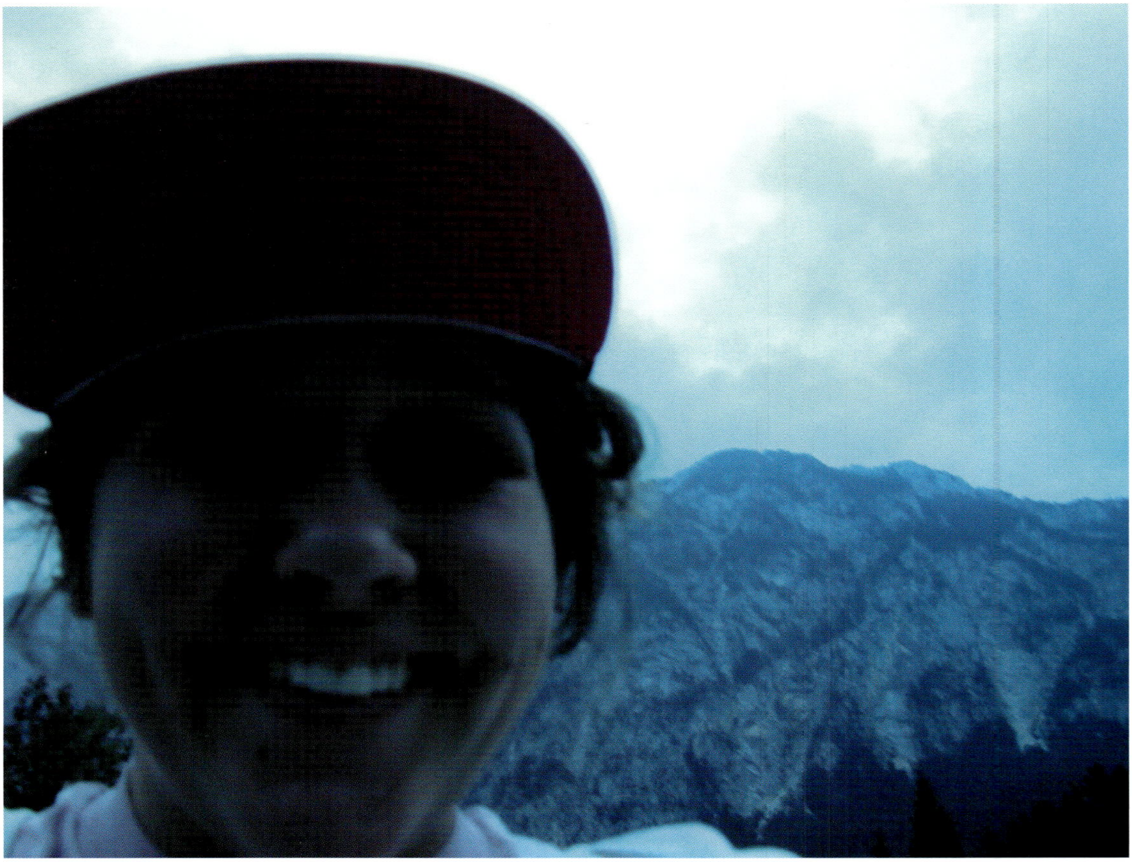

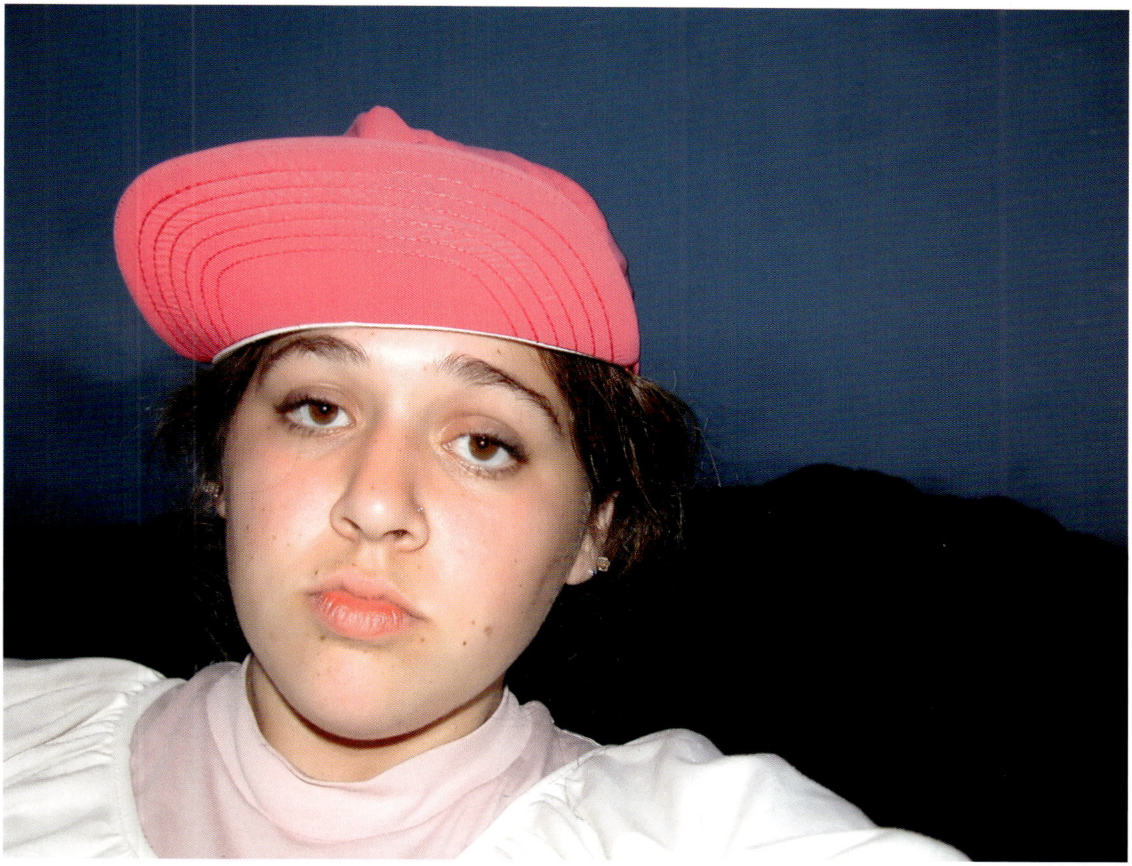

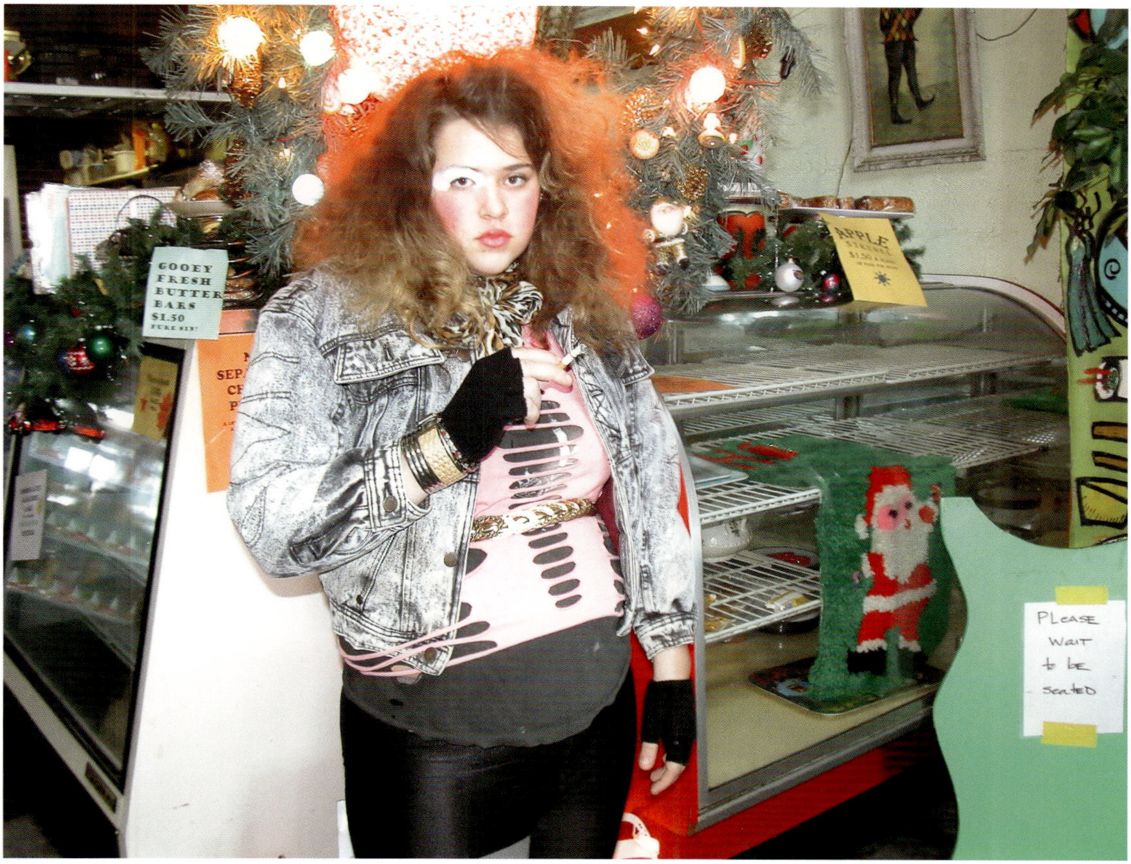
GOOEY
FRESH
BUTTER
BARS
$1.50
APPLE
PLEASE
WAIT
to be
seated

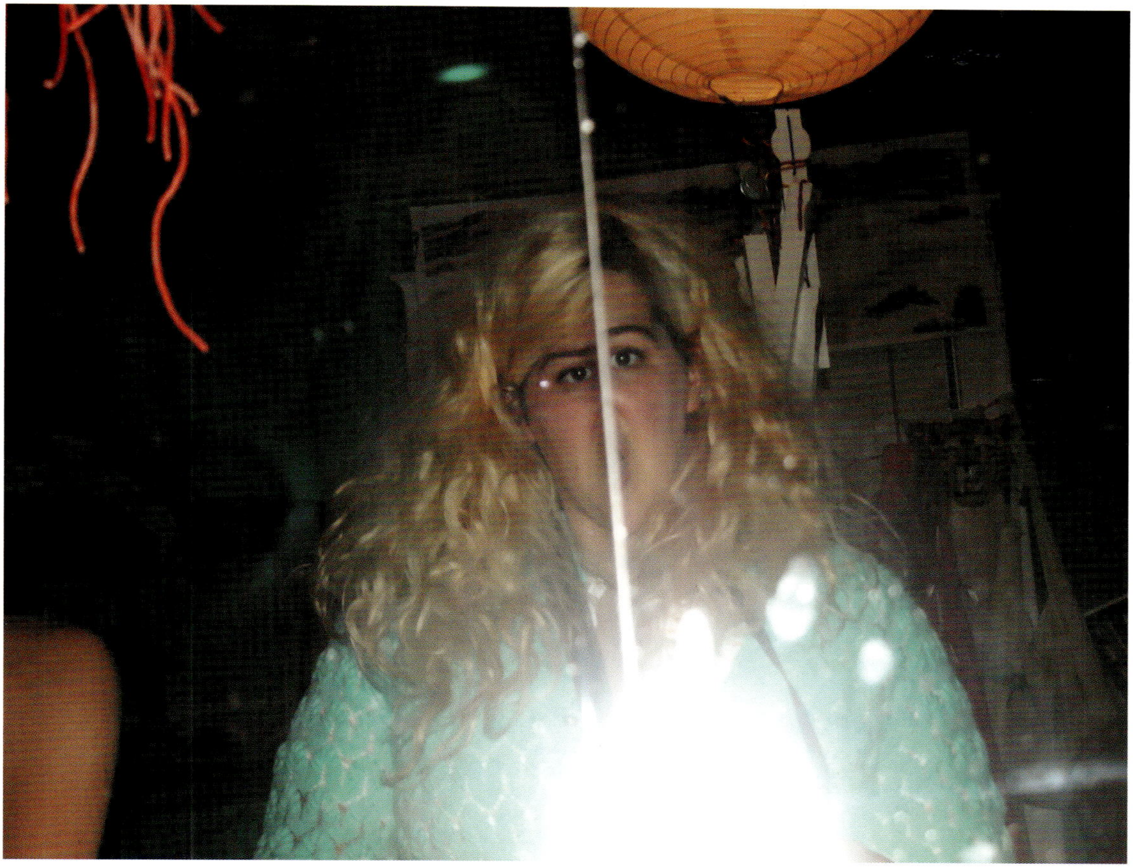

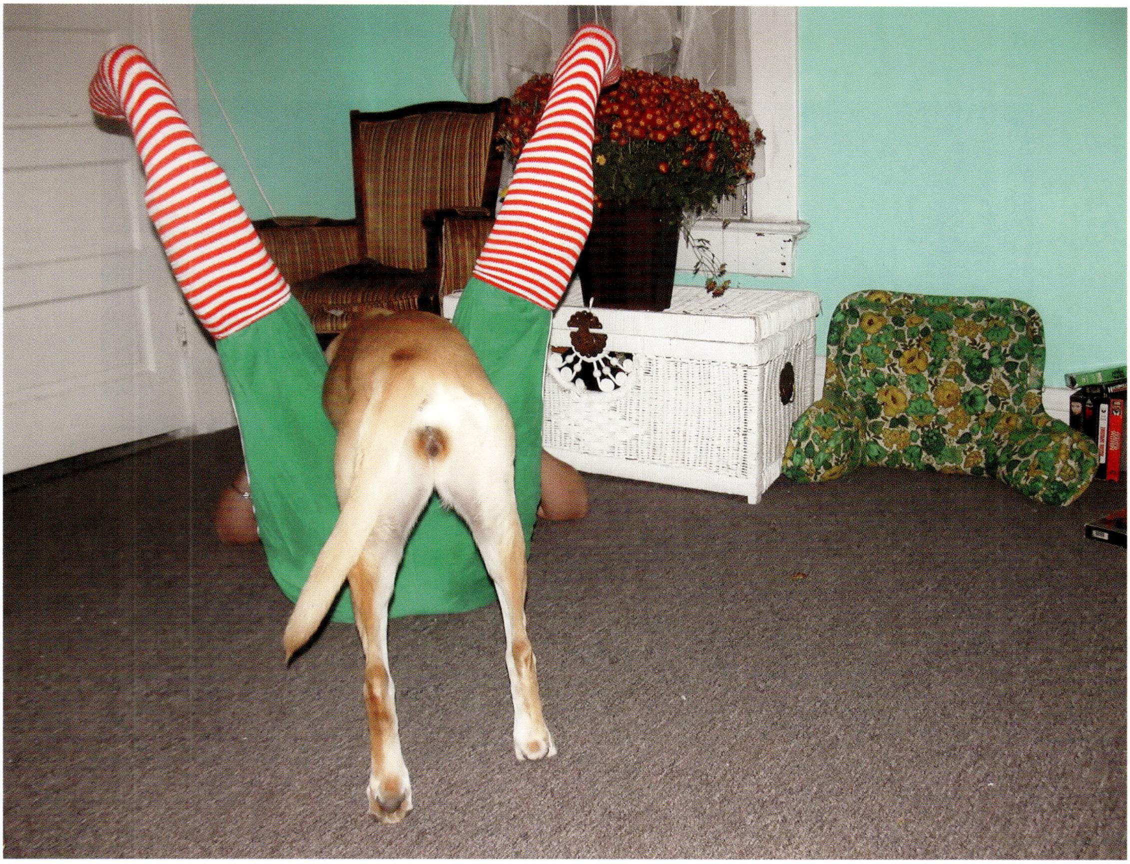

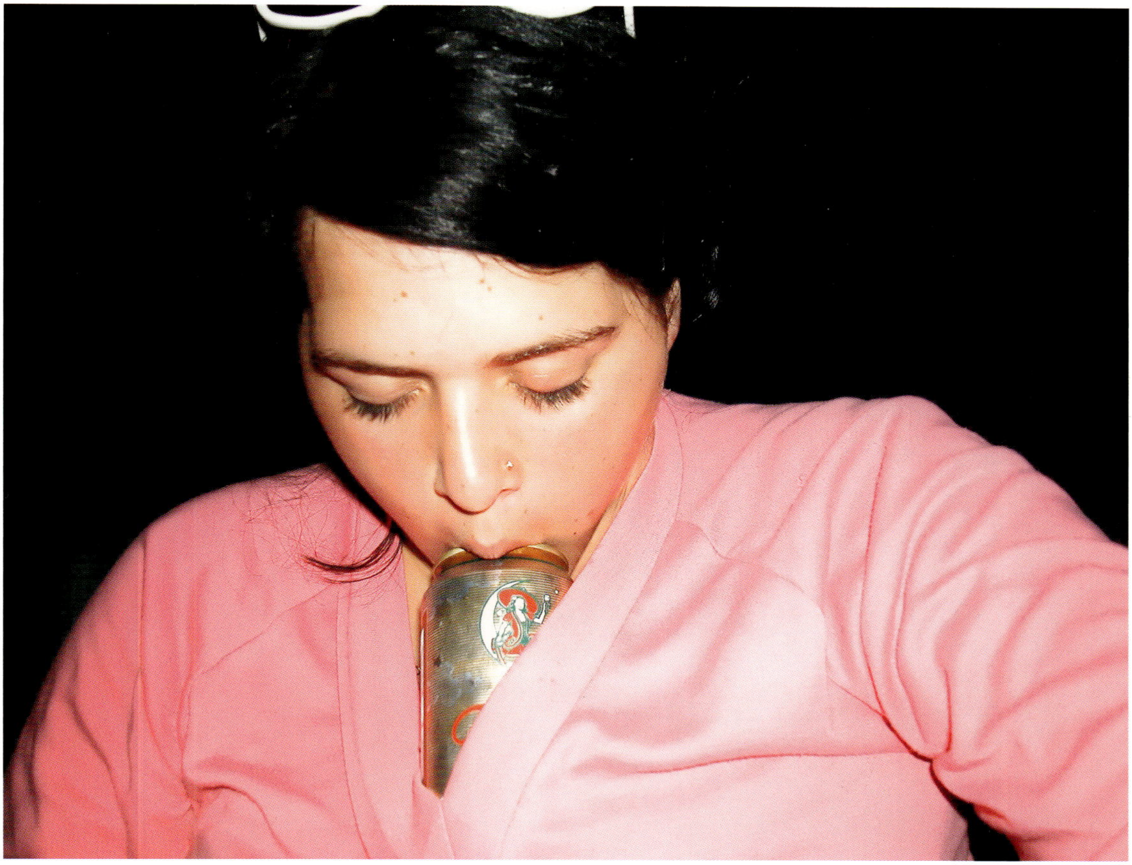

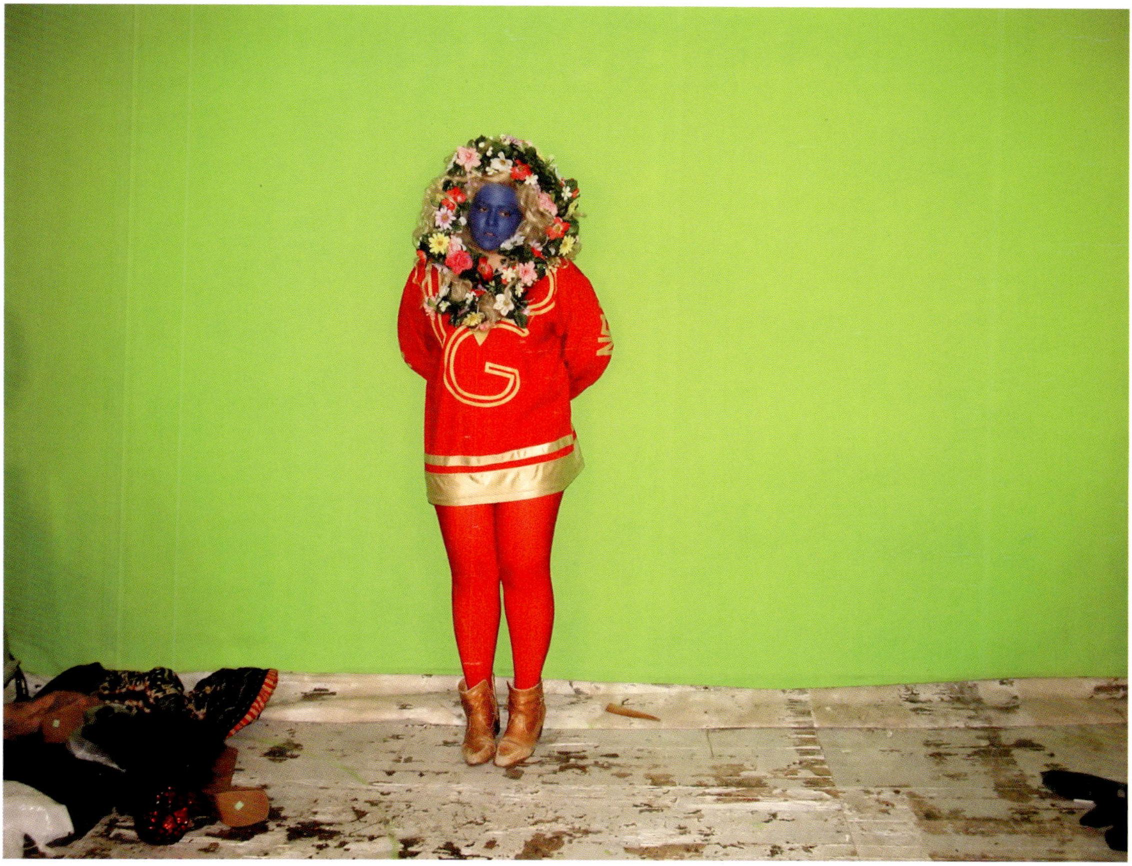

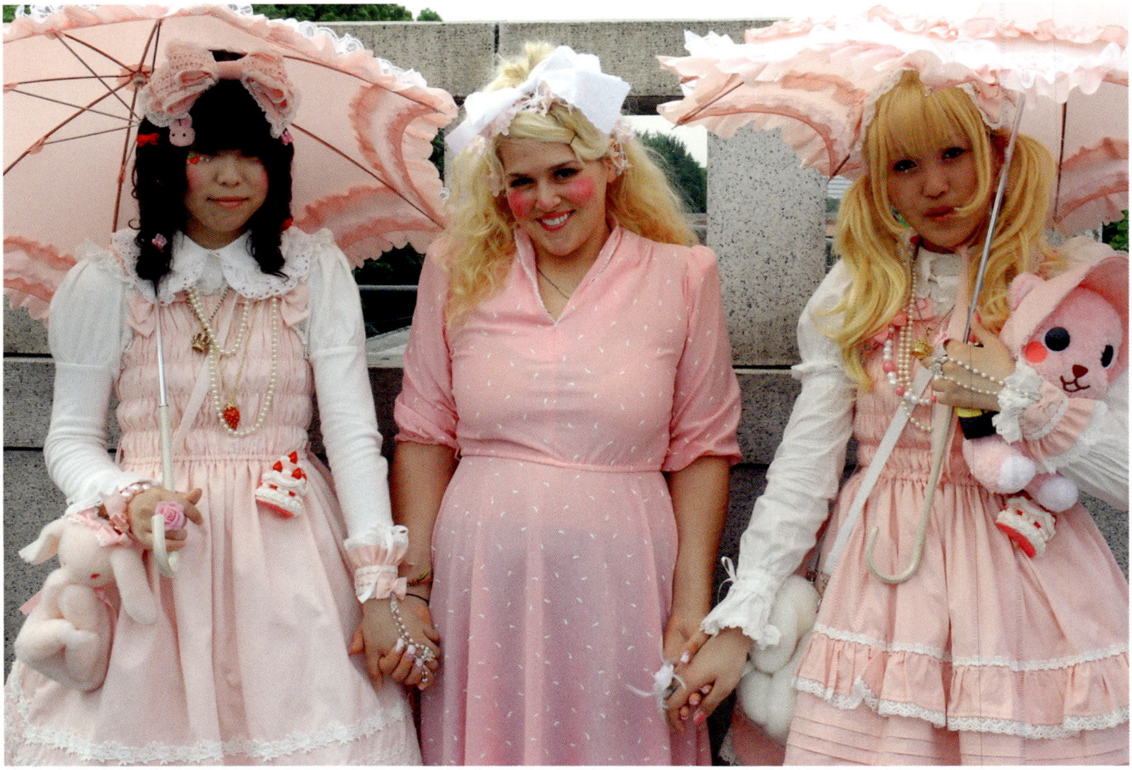

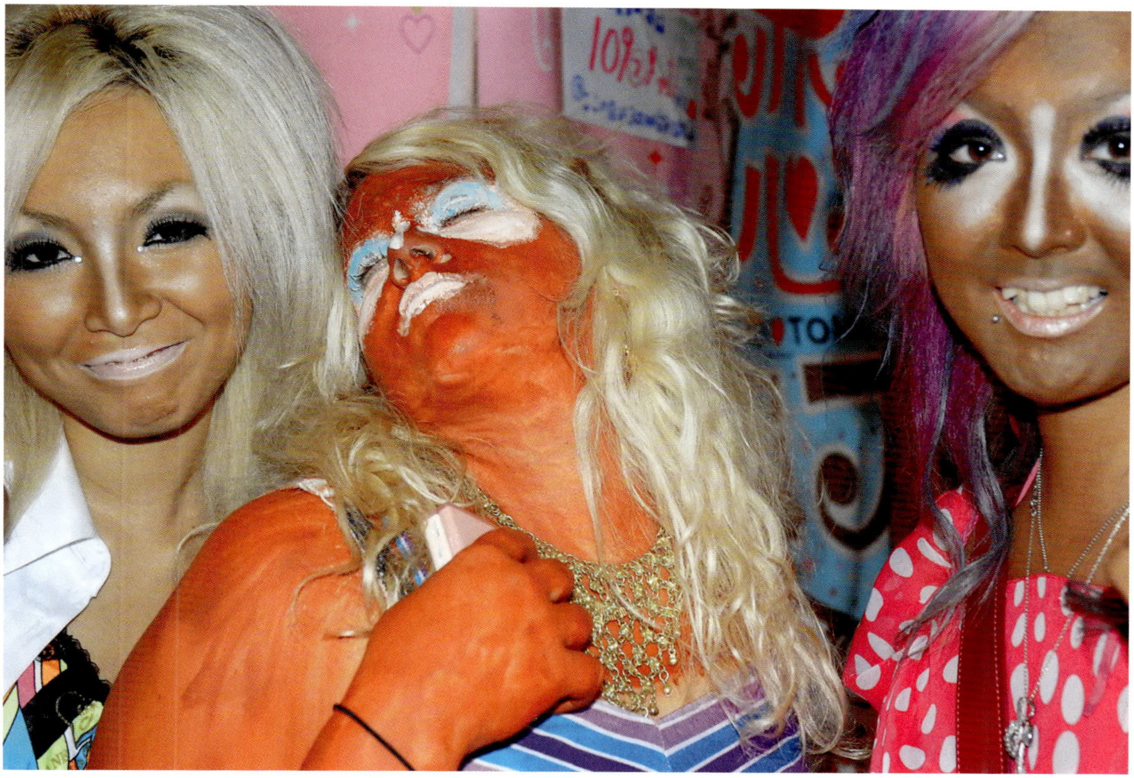

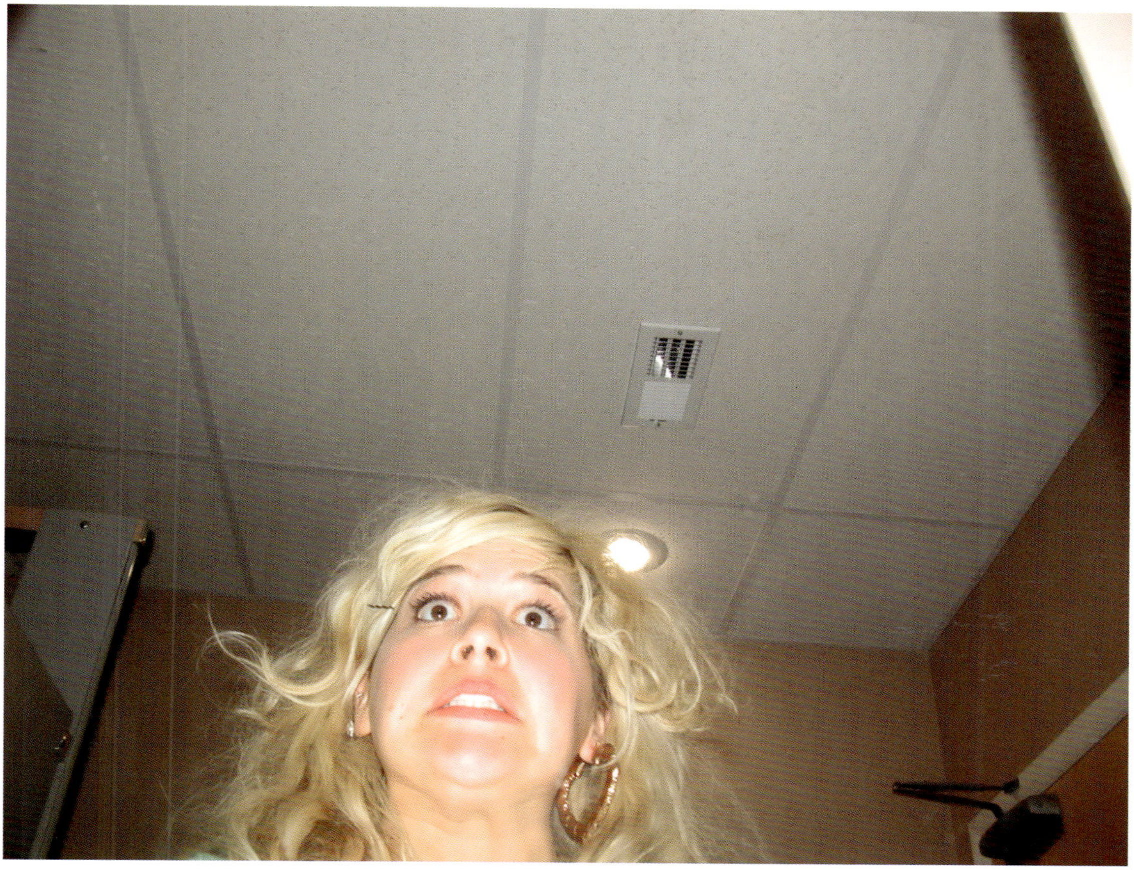

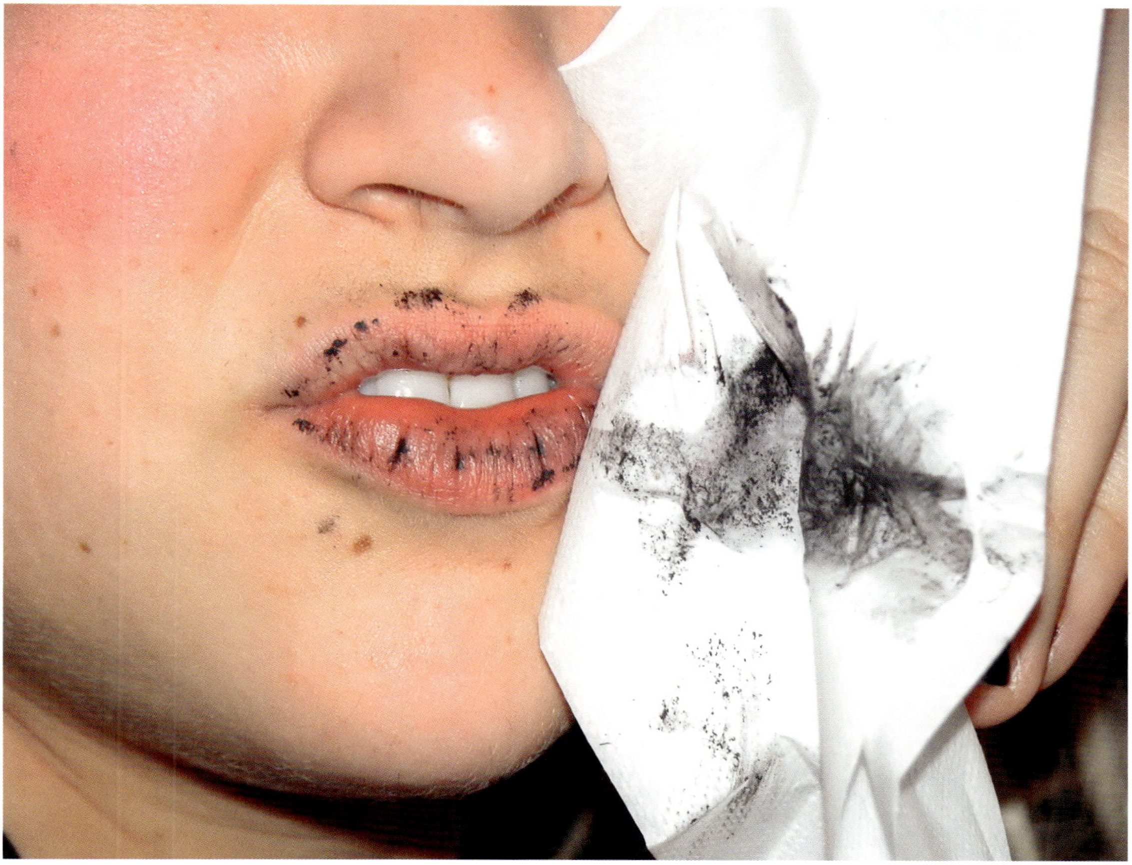

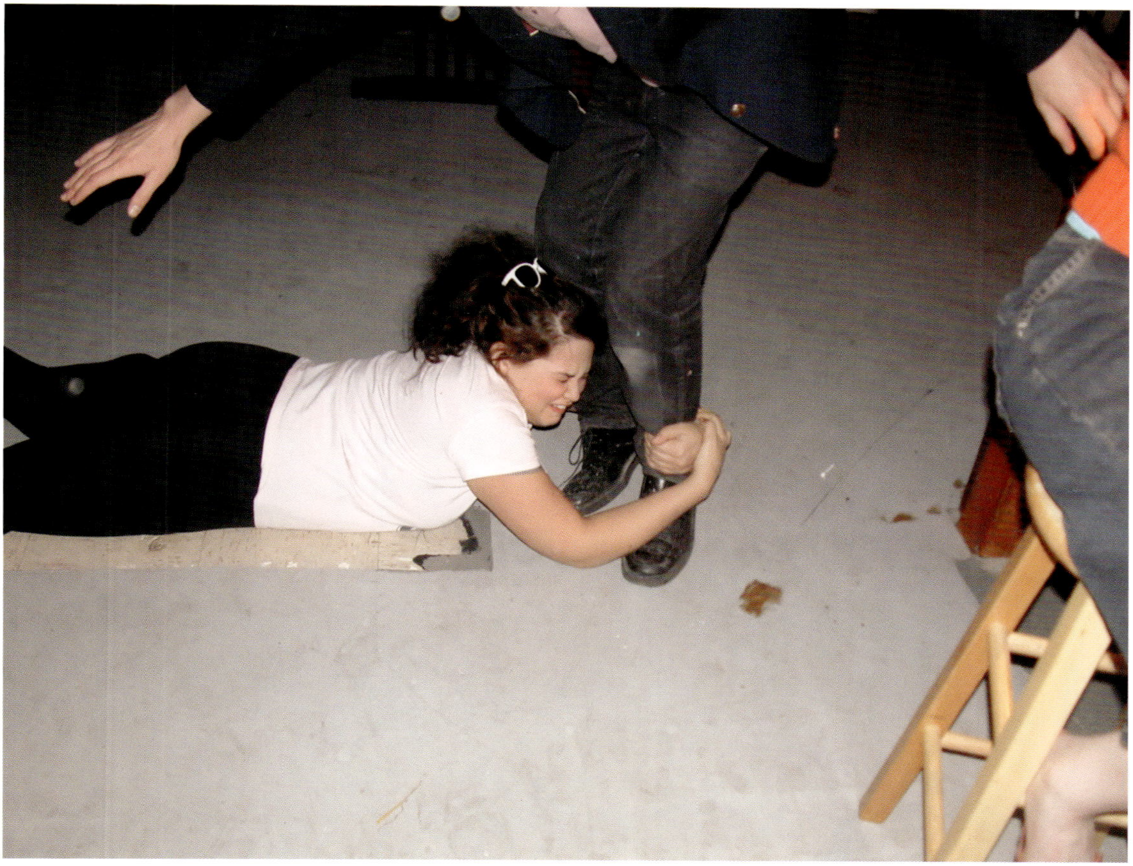

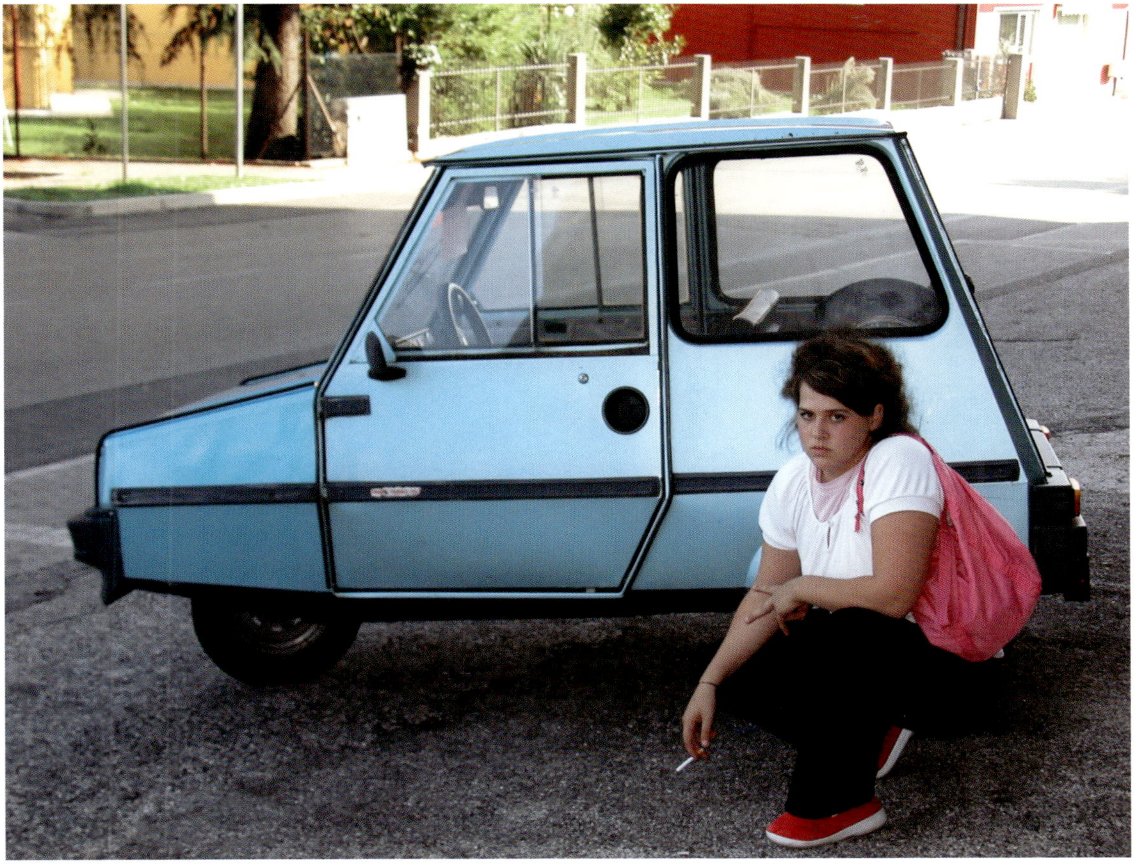

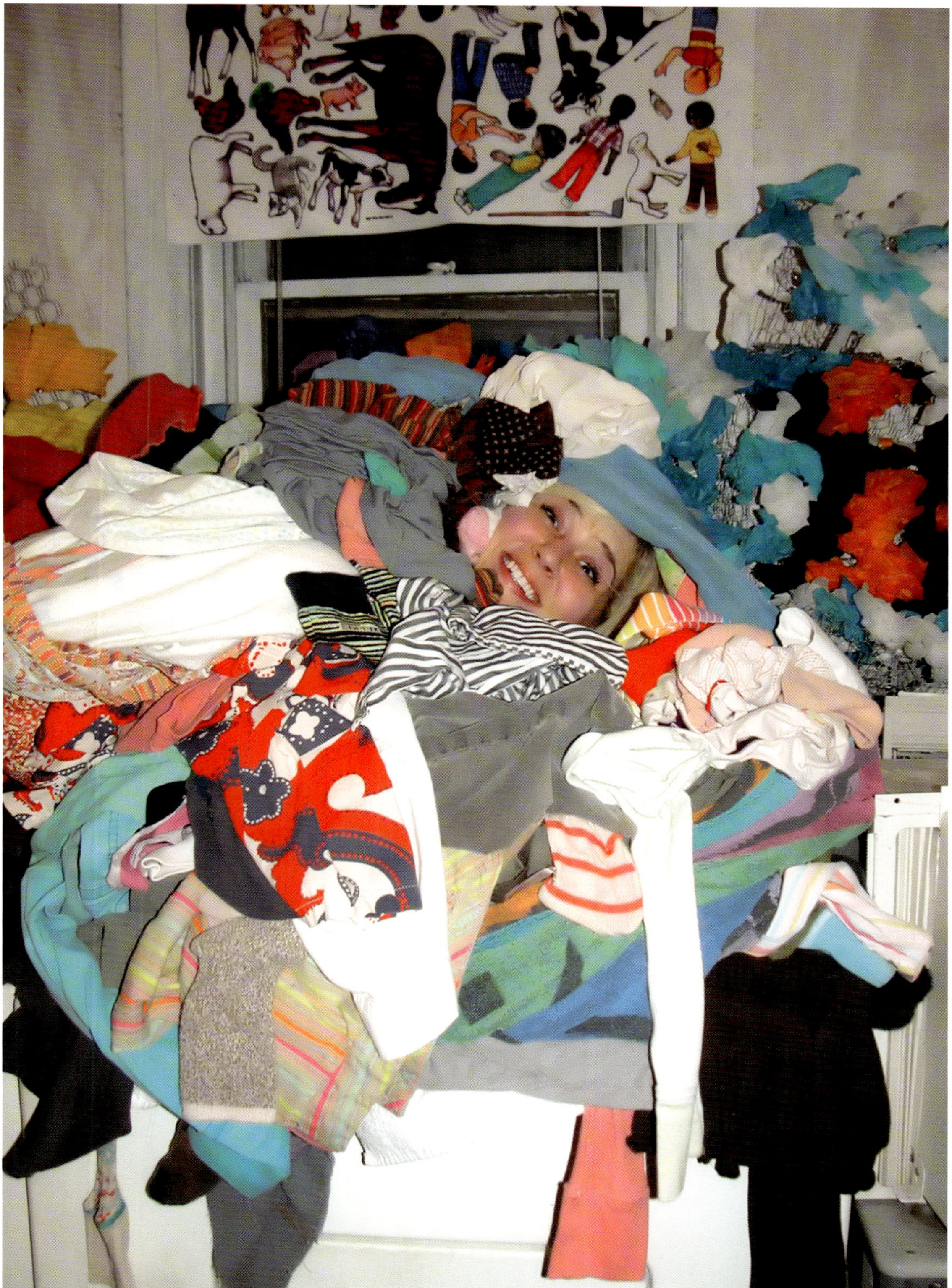

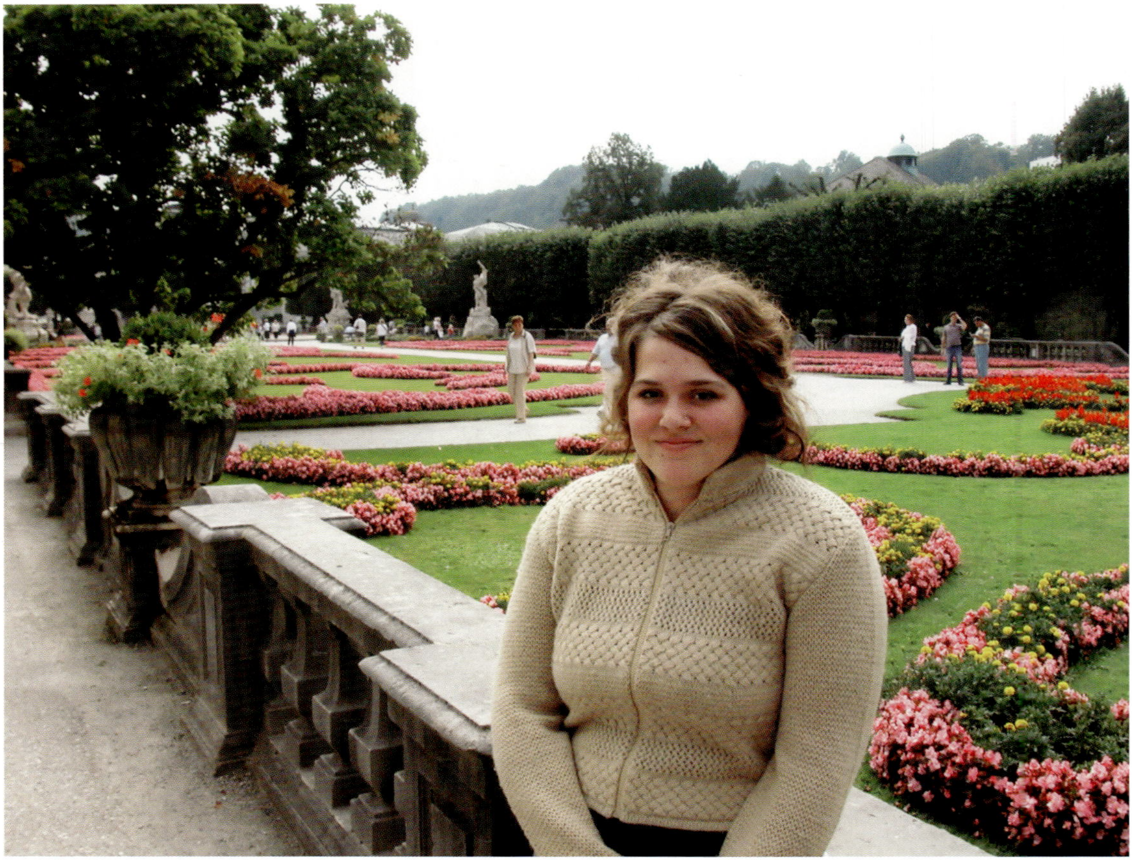

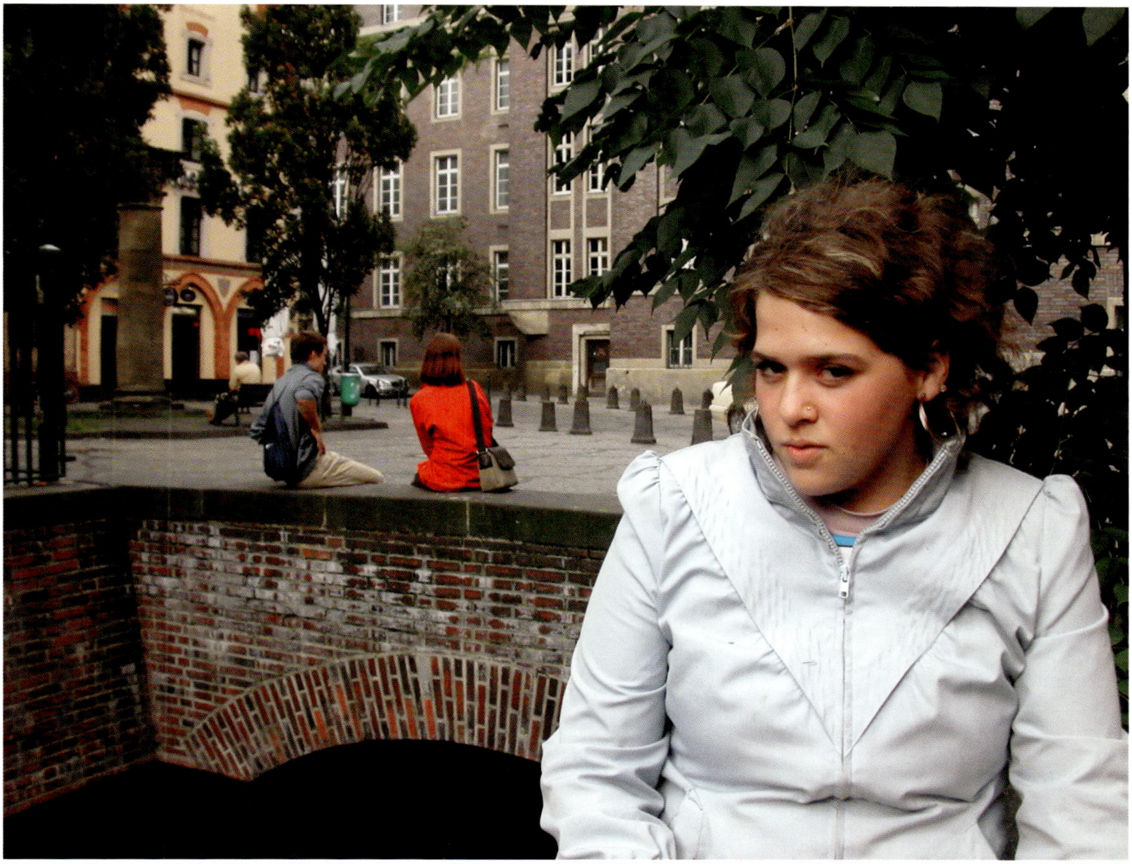

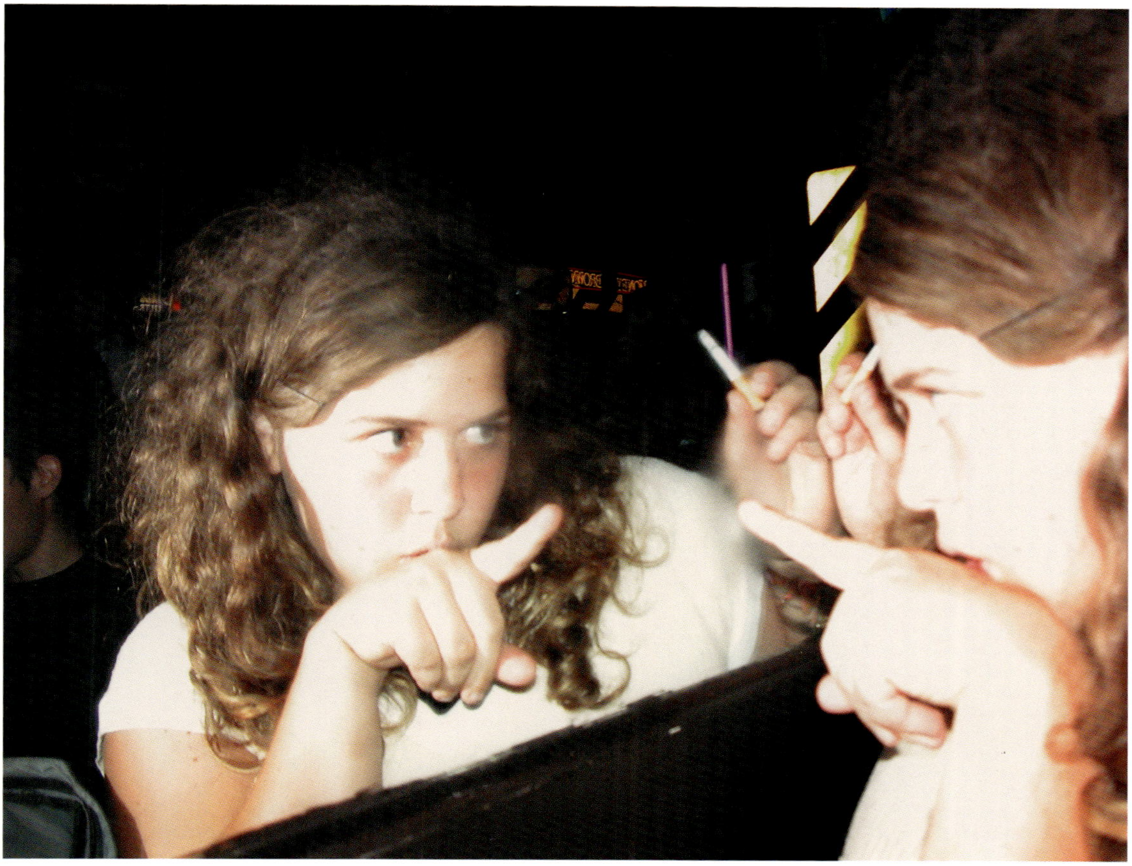

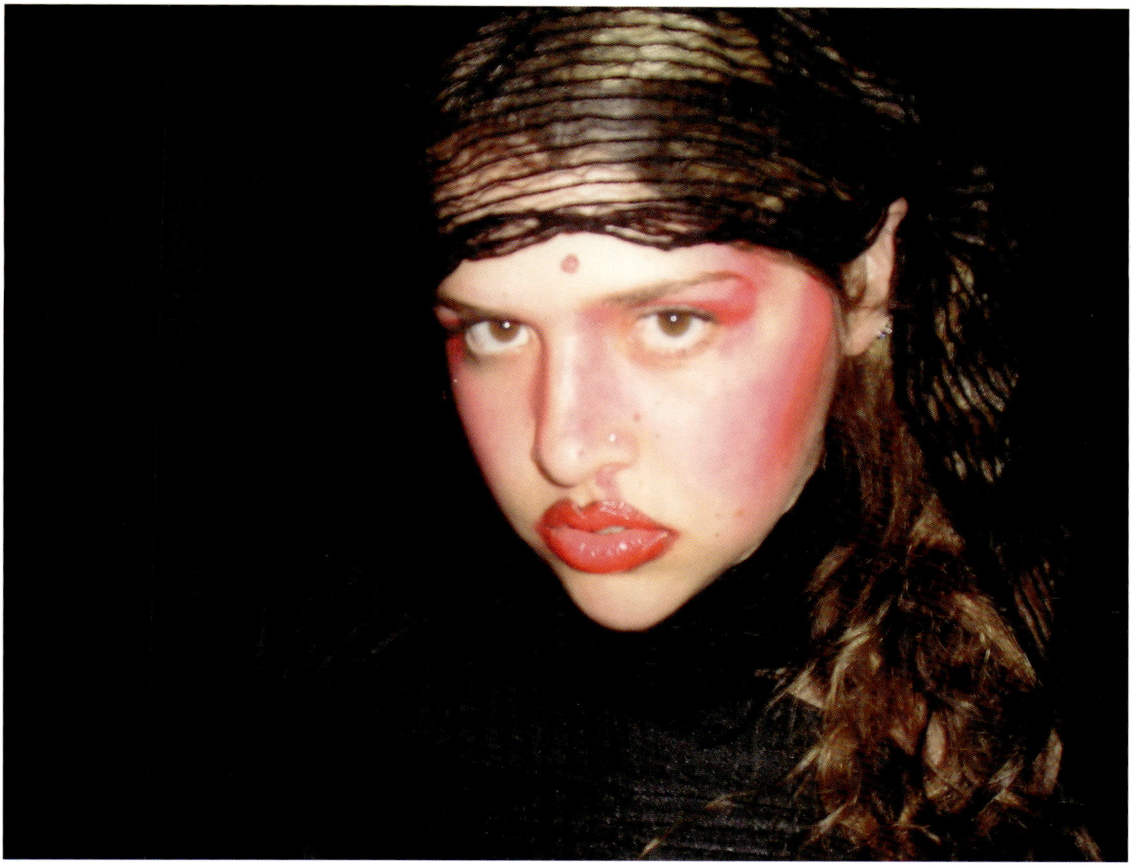

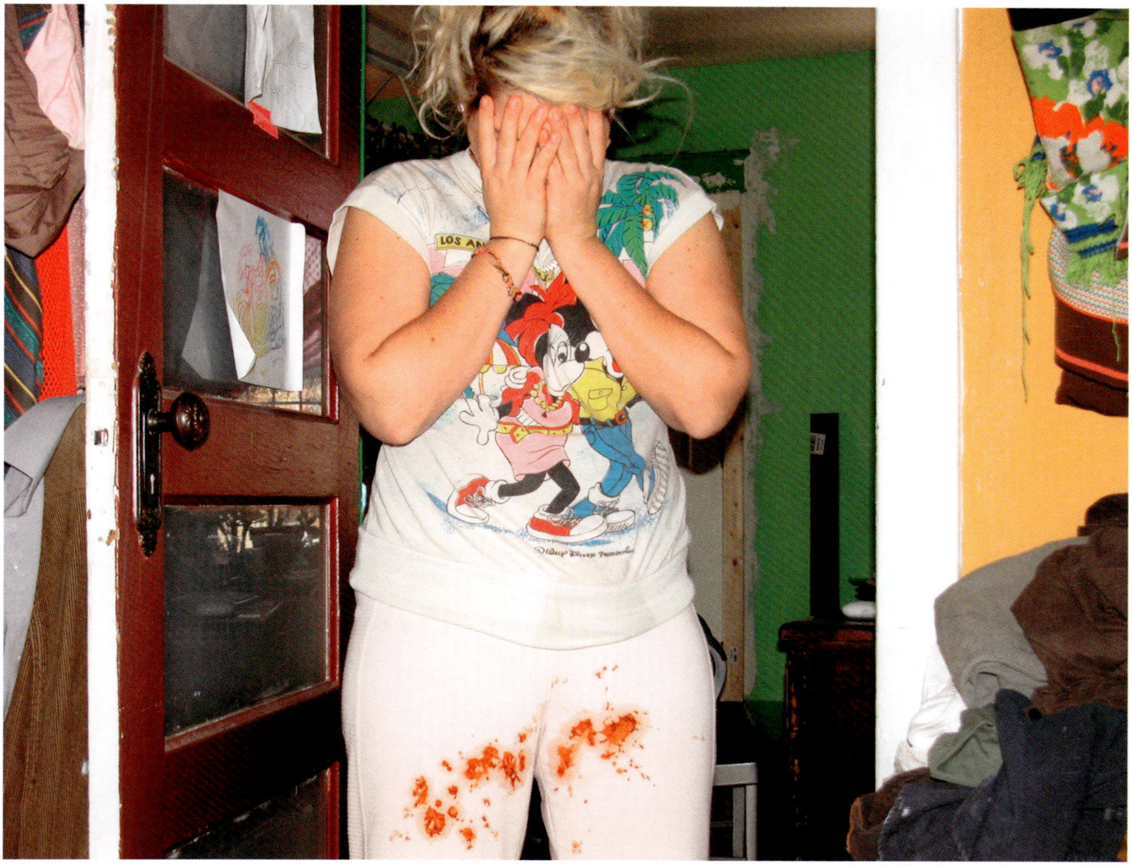

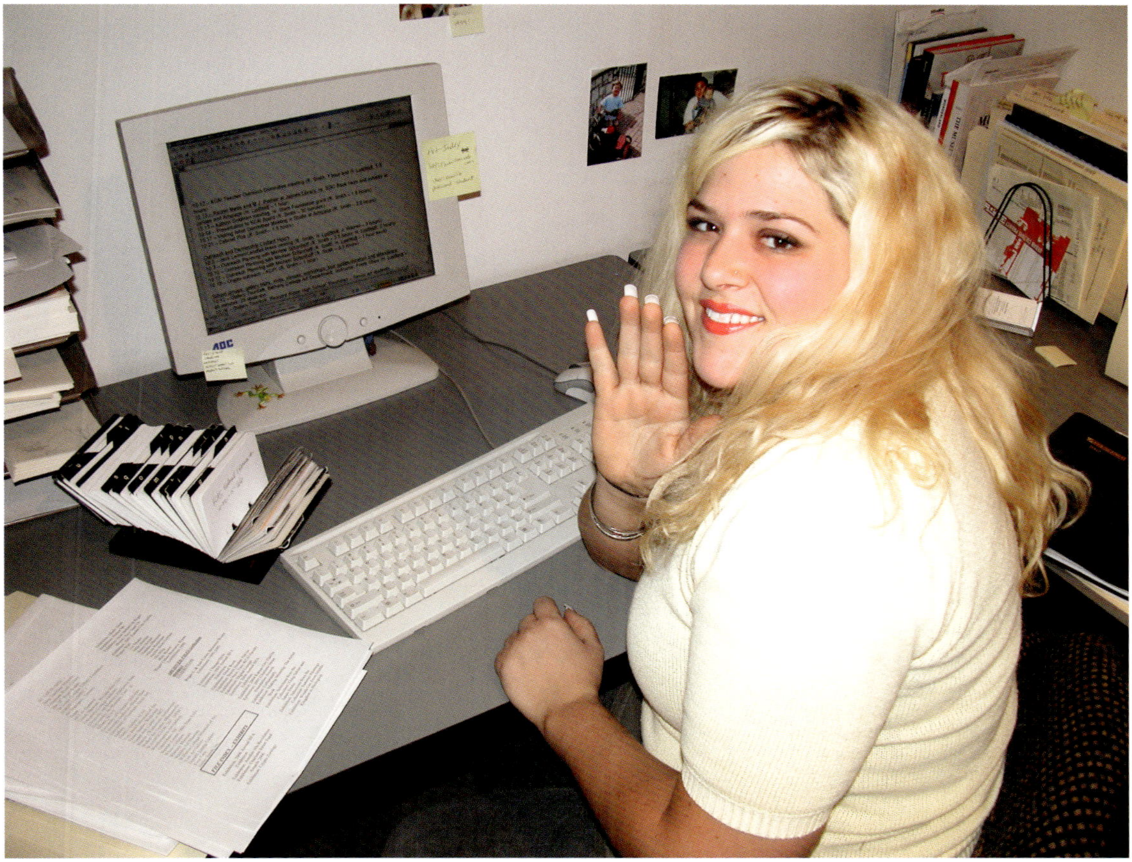

PLATES

27 *Untitled (Self Portrait, Red and Flowers, Tokyo)*, 2007

28 *Untitled (Self Portrait, Ice Fishing)*, 2005

29 *Untitled (Self Portrait, Tupac)*, 2006

30 *Untitled (Self Portrait, Normal Girl, Racquetball)*, 2006

31 *Untitled (Self Portrait, Normal Girl in Car)*, 2006

32 *Untitled (Self Portrait, Alps #1)*, 2004

33 *Untitled (Self Portrait, Alps #2)*, 2004

34 *Untitled (Self Portrait, Succotash Punk)*, 2005

35 *Untitled (Self Portrait, Split Mirror)*, 2006

36 *Untitled (Self Portrait, Percy's Butt)*, 2005

37 *Untitled (Self Portrait, Pink and Beer)*, 2003

38 *Untitled (Self Portrait, Blue Face /Green Screen)*, 2008

39 *Untitled (Self Portrait, Doll Girls, Tokyo)*, 2007

40 *Untitled (Self Portrait, Yamamba Girls, Tokyo)*, 2007

41 *Untitled (Self Portrait in Mirror)*, 2007

42 *Untitled (Self Portrait, Black Lips)*, 2007

43 *Untitled (Self Portrait, Jackson's Legs)*, 2004

44 *Untitled (Self Portrait with Tri-car, Italy)*, 2004

45 *Untitled (Self Portrait, Laundry)*, 2006

46 *Untitled (Self Portrait, Flowers, Austria)*, 2004

47 *Untitled (Self Portrait, River, Germany)*, 2004

48 *Untitled (Self Portrait, News Room Mirror)*, 2006

49 *Untitled (Self Portrait, Y-not)*, 2005

50 *Untitled (Self Portrait, Chili)*, 2008

51 *Untitled (Self Portrait, Normal Girl, Artspace)*, 2006

ACKNOWLEDGMENTS

This book is lovingly dedicated to my family (Mom, Dad, Lindsay, and Matthew) and my wonderful friends: Peggy, Patrick, Cody, Matt, Alex, Heather, Kate, Seth, Amy, Hesse, Naoko, Chloe, Sean, Ari, and Marcus. Biggest thanks ever to Tim Barber and my idol, Roseanne Barr.

Front cover: *Untitled (Self Portrait, Red and Flowers, Tokyo)*, 2007

Edited and designed by Tim Barber
Aperture Editor: Michael Famighetti
Publisher: Lesley A. Martin
Production: Matthew Pimm
Work Scholar: Carolyn Deuschle

Funded in part by The Lighton International Artists Exchange Program, A Project of The Kansas City Artists Coalition. Images courtesy of Higher Pictures.

Edition of 1,000
Printed in Singapore

Library of Congress Control Number: 2008928796
ISBN 978-1-59711-085-3

Aperture Foundation books are available in North America through:
D.A.P./Distributed Art Publishers
155 Sixth Avenue, 2nd Floor, New York, N.Y. 10013
Phone: (212) 627-1999, Fax: (212) 627-9484

Aperture Foundation books are distributed outside North America by:
Thames & Hudson
181A High Holborn, London WC1V 7QX, United Kingdom
Phone: + 44 20 7845 5000, Fax: + 44 20 7845 5055
Email: sales@thameshudson.co.uk

aperturefoundation

547 West 27th Street
New York, N.Y. 10001
www.aperture.org

The purpose of Aperture Foundation, a non-profit organization, is to advance photography in all its forms and to foster the exchange of ideas among audiences worldwide.